How to Write a Paragraph Using Study Skills

5 Simple Steps to Writing Powerful Paragraphs

Stephanie Reeves

Copyright © Stephanie Reeves, 2022 - All rights reserved.

The content contained within this book may not be reproduced, duplicated, or transmitted without direct written permission from the author or the publisher.

Under no circumstances will any blame or legal responsibility be held against the publisher, or author, for any damages, reparation, or monetary loss due to the information contained within this book, either directly or indirectly.

Legal Notice:

This book is copyright protected. It is only for personal use. You cannot amend, distribute, sell, use, quote, or paraphrase any part, or the content within this book, without the consent of the author or publisher.

Disclaimer Notice:

Please note the information contained within this document is for educational and entertainment purposes only. All effort has been executed to present accurate, up-to-date, reliable, complete information. No warranties of any kind are declared or implied. Readers acknowledge that the author is not engaged in the rendering of legal, financial, medical, or professional advice. The content within this book has been derived from various sources. Please consult a licensed professional before attempting any techniques outlined in this book.

By reading this document, the reader agrees that under no circumstances is the author responsible for any losses, direct or indirect, that are incurred as a result of the use of the information contained within this document, including, but not limited to, errors, omissions, or inaccuracies.

Contents

Bonus!	v
Introduction	vii
1. Where Do Students Go Wrong With Writing!?	1
2. What Are Study Skills and How Do I Create Them?	20
3. Forming a Study Plan	43
4. Additional Tips for Students With Other Needs	52
5. Step 1: Understanding the Functions and Purpose of a Paragraph	61
6. Step 2: Identifying Paragraphs and Recognizing the Structure of a Good One	71
7. Step 3: Composing Your Powerful Paragraph Using Study Skills	98
8. Step 4: Fleshing out Your Paragraph Without Fluff or Waffling	119
9. Step 5: Using Study Skills To Proofread and Edit Your Paragraph to Perfection	135
10. Applying Your Newfound Skills to Longer Writing Tasks	148

Conclusion	167
Bonus! - '5 Habits that Make Learning Any Subject Quicker and Easier'	171
About the Author	173
Leave a review!	175
Glossary	177
References	187

If you're interested in receiving a free copy of our guide to the '*5 Habits that make Learning any Subject Quicker and Easier*', scan the QR code below!

Introduction

How many hours have you sat staring into space, hoping inspiration will strike? Whether it is an empty page on your computer screen or a blank piece of paper lying before you, we all understand the feeling of uncertainty and frustration. The ideas that felt so inspiring half an hour ago just don't seem to work out once you start writing about them. On top of that, every time you reread your writing, you have this sinking feeling that the project isn't going well. You might even begin to wonder whether you'll ever excel at writing.

Sound familiar? We've all been there, stressing out over writing that email, cover letter, blog post, or essay with the deadline fast approaching. Even something as 'simple' as a paragraph might feel like an impossible task. You might find yourself wondering, "Is there an easy way to go about this?"

The answer, I'm happy to say, is YES!

Facing Off With a Blank Page

Are you a parent trying to figure out a way to help your child with a writing assignment? Or maybe you're a teacher trying to make writing fun. Perhaps even a student who's struggling to put two sentences together for an essay. You might even be a working professional who wants to expand their business with a strong social media presence. Whoever you are, the good news is, with the proper approach to studying and writing, you'll begin to excel with five simple steps!

While practice makes perfect, you can make the path to perfection easier. More often than not, the obstacle to a good paragraph ends up being a matter of time management, study skills, and proper understanding of what a paragraph entails. Thankfully, there are many tricks, tips, and techniques to help you not only write better but plan and study effectively, maximize your time, and ensure solid research along the way.

Whether your page is blank or filled with notes and ideas, it's time to get you on the path to writing success!

My Commitment To Excellence

I firmly believe that everyone experiences their own unique learning journey, and I recognize that the path to great writing isn't easy for everyone. However, foundational steps can empower any potential writer who seeks to improve how they communicate. With these tips and techniques, the blank page, and daunting task of an essay, are easily conquered. Using the right tools, you will improve your abilities regardless of your starting point.

My background in psychology and psychoanalytic psychotherapy—for children and adolescents—provides me with a unique perspective on education. As an educator and child care provider, I support students and families who struggle with learning. I believe that, regardless of emotional, educational, and developmental needs, my students can achieve their academic goals and become great communicators.

Introduction

Navigating a Path to Success

Since we rely on the written word as much as the spoken, writing well is often a cornerstone to success in life. I want to encourage and empower you to try out the simple, practical steps provided. In this book, you'll discover the tools to improve your writing skills in a way that you can apply to all facets of your life. It isn't just about understanding how to write a good college paper, but also how to communicate clearly and easily online, at work, or at home. Some of the foundational skills introduced in this book, such as self-awareness and positivity, can be used in other areas of your life as well.

You will learn how to assess your strengths and weaknesses as a writer, form better study habits, recognize your study skills, and understand what role a paragraph plays in communication. After that, you will practice writing, editing, and proofreading using various prompts. By the end of the book, you'll have two or three writing samples polished and ready for your audience. Let's get started!

Chapter 1
Where Do Students Go Wrong With Writing!?

Looking out my window, I smile at the promise of clear weather. The sky is blue, the sun is shining, and it looks like it's going to be a perfect day for an outing with my friend. We had decided to try out a new restaurant. Because the route is unfamiliar, I pop on Google Maps and follow the GPS voice to the destination. I must input my current address and the restaurant's address to set it up. Once both points are set, I can choose which road map to travel.

Hm... Does this sound familiar? I bet you can see where this is going. Just like traveling, preparing for a new goal or project, writing or otherwise, requires an understanding of your present position and future destination. Before committing yourself to a plan, it's always a good idea to take stock of where you stand. For example, if you want to cook better, you have to think about the common mistakes you're making in the kitchen right now. Or, if you collect stamps, you need to know what stamps you already have in your collection and what ones you still need to get.

In the same way, if you want to improve your writing, you will first need to assess yourself. What are your strengths and weaknesses as a writer? Where do you feel most challenged? What is standing in the way of you writing a powerful paragraph, blog, or essay? Once you understand the answers to these questions, you can plot a better path to the results you're looking for!

Consider the Challenges of Writing

Do you have that friend who doesn't think writing is such a big deal? They might be the type who say something like, "What's the matter? Just write!" That's so frustrating and unhelpful, right? After all, most of us have to develop our writing skills the way athletes need to train. It takes time and energy!

For each of us, there are different challenges found in writing. Some of us might find the idea part difficult, whereas others might feel like the actual writing is hard to keep focused on. When you're struggling with one or more challenges in writing, it feels all too easy to give up. Let's look at some common issues that crop up during the writing process.

Where Have the Good Ideas Gone?

Whether you are writing a blog or trying to answer an essay question, you might not know how to move forward at the most fundamental stage; thinking up a good idea. The more freedom or openness you have, the more discouraging this stage might become. After all, with less restriction comes less guidance, which means more pressure on the creative juices needed to plan your writing task. When performance is linked to creativity in this way, the wellspring of inspiration can unexpectedly run dry. On the other hand, if you're attempting to answer an essay question, you may suddenly feel you don't understand what's being asked. It can be very discouraging to realize that you might not have all the information needed to move forward with the project, so where do you go from here?

The good news is that you don't have to be stuck in concept creation limbo forever. There are quite a few methods to jumpstart inspiration and set you on the path to a great blog or essay:

- Discuss the question or material with your teacher, fellow student, parent, or friend.
- Research! Research! Research!
- Brainstorm using lists or bubble-type mind maps.

As a teacher or parent, if you are trying to help your students or child to overcome this stage, you can facilitate a better understanding of the topic or set up a brainstorming session. First, review the material and then follow this up with independent research using various sources. When the budding writer can talk about their topic comfortably and answer questions, they are more than likely at a stage they feel comfortable enough to start writing.

Dangers of Distracted Driving

Like driving a car, the safest way to get from Point A to Point B is to maintain your focus. That being said, more often than not, there are things in life that are sure to distract us. Some of those things are necessary, such as eating, resting, or spending time with friends and family. However, many distractions like social media are less than productive, breaking your focus and workflow, which often worsens with a deadline looming. Feeling pressured might be enough to ignore distractions, but stress is just as likely to demotivate us while shifting our focus toward feel-good activities that don't help get the job done. Still, you can overcome this problem by creating a space to focus with minimal interruptions. With a quiet, solitary work environment, you can maximize the preparation you've made for your writing session. Consider these tips to help increase your focus!

- Try out a concentration or focus meditation.
- Set your word processor settings to reduce distractions.
- Use an app that tracks your work hours and reminds you to take breaks.

For teachers and parents, if your student or child is still struggling with feeling distracted, make sure they've had a break, a breath of fresh air, or a change of activity. Something as simple as stretching, or going for a walk, can help bring perspective and renewed energy. Review their notes and research materials as a lack of preparation may encourage your young writers to avoid the task at hand. Once you've assessed the cause of their distractions or why maintaining focus remains a problem, you'll be better equipped to empower them and get them back on track.

So You Want it To Be Over Already?

I think it's safe to say that we've all had that moment where we are sitting by a window writing something and wishing we were outside. Anywhere feels better than here. It's the same feeling we get when facing those mundane tasks that need to get done. We might be doing housework, homework, or work at home when suddenly, we just want to do something else. How do we usually respond to this abrupt desire? We work faster! Unfortunately, powering through our work more often than not doesn't mean we're completing the project or chore well. Typically, increasing speed decreases the quality of our work. Impatience causes a poor result requiring us to spend even more time fixing our mistakes. It's crucial, therefore, to take your time and keep focused. If you find yourself feeling bogged down during the writing process, take a deep breath and let yourself know it's OK to slow down. You can also ensure your writing goes smoothly by following these simple tips:

- Write up a super detailed outline based on good research.
- Reread your work at set intervals.
- Plan small breaks.

Before sitting your student or child down to write a project, make sure all tools necessary for a smooth writing experience are prepared. This means you should double-check their research material, outline, and writing schedule. Reassure your students by providing a healthy reward system to improve focus and motivation. On top of that, encourage beginner writers to reread their work or take a break. With your help, beginner writers can learn how to pace themselves properly, which will result in a better mindset and foundation for solid writing.

When You Just Want To Netflix and Chill

Whenever it's time to sit down and deal with something I'm not super excited about, it's incredible how suddenly motivated I am to complete other tasks.

Sometimes I can't even hide the fact I'm avoiding what needs to get done. On those days, I cave to the lure of my couch and just Netflix and chill. I can say, from experience, that the writing process is, most easily, disrupted by procrastination. The delay or putting something off until later. If you have caught yourself saying something like, "I'll do it tomorrow," you are likely procrastinating. We've all struggled with it, although it may look different from person to person. Some procrastinators tell themselves that they like to work under the pressure of close deadlines. While others feel as though their new ideas are distracting them from their work at hand, making completing their old projects impossible. Whatever the reasons, procrastination never gets you to where you are going. Get out of the procrastination rut! Try these techniques to refocus and find motivation:

- Break your project down into small steps that you can achieve.
- Treat yourself with a reward when you complete your first goal.
- Write new ideas and projects down in an inspiration notebook or on sticky notes to deal with later.

Grappling with procrastination is familiar to us all; however, it's not easy to help someone struggling with this problem during a writing project. As a teacher or parent, you may need to collaborate with the writer to ensure they're taking breaks, as necessary, and keeping on task. If your student or child is battling to complete a project, allow them a time of introspection to ask themselves what they're avoiding. Once they understand the true reason behind their delay tactics, you'll be better able to walk them through the problem.

Putting Out the Dumpster Fire

Getting started and keeping on task is difficult enough for many beginner writers. Even when the written project is complete, the battle is not yet over. To produce a polished piece, you must edit and proofread your work. This step is challenging when the first draft looks like a dumpster fire. If discouraged by the amount of work remaining, or the state of the writing project, it may be too easy for you to run a spell-checker and leave it at that, but how much potential gets lost as a result? Editing and proofreading require an eye for detail, a fresh perspective, and a solid knowledge of writing techniques. If you're already struggling to write a paragraph, it will be no surprise if you miss out on errors or fail to correct issues in the text. Even if you're a decent writer, it can be hard to get your work looking and sounding great. What is one supposed to do?

- Read your piece of writing backward.
- Get a reliable peer student, tutor, or parent to look over the project.
- Set your writing aside for a day or two, then go back to look at it.

When checking the first draft, peer editing is often a go-to technique. In first-time writing projects, teachers can schedule peer-editing tasks to enhance learning. Giving time for the students to turn in their first draft for reliable feedback helps you help them. On the other hand, tutors and parents can also assist young writers in forming healthy time management skills by allowing for appropriate feedback on their first drafts. This draft might look discouraging, but with proper support, struggling writers will feel more encouraged about the writing process as a whole and recognize editing as their safety net.

How to Write a Paragraph Using Study Skills

Writing provides even the most seasoned students and content writers with many challenges. Consider every step of the way. The writer should remain focused, motivated, and productive. However, at times we set ourselves up for failure by not taking into account the parts of the writing process where we struggle. On top of that, when we fail to understand our strengths and weaknesses as writers, we end up not recognizing which part of the writing process is tripping us up.

Know Yourself as a Writer

What kind of writer are you? How do you approach studying and research? Which part of writing challenges you the most? By answering these kinds of questions, you will discover your problem with writing. Could it be a distracting study environment? An inconsistent schedule or missing information on the process of writing? It's time to figure out what is standing in the way of your best writing ever!

Your Strengths and Weaknesses

Whether you're planning, writing, or polishing your written project, you will find some parts of the writing process easier than others. Let's have a look at some potential strengths you might have when it comes to writing!

Innovative Concepts vs. Vague Ideas

Are you able to see patterns or think up new ideas? If so, you may have the gift of forming new topics to discuss, meaning you can devise a brand-new argument, which is sure to draw in an audience. Often, the difference between a grade A and a grade B paper is simply the level of innovation used in addressing the essay question. If you find yourself always jotting down ideas, chances are you have the potential to ideate original thoughts to write about!

Strong Research Abilities vs. Lack of Good Content

No essay is complete without solid research as it provides the foundation upon which your thesis stands. Do you love looking up information and verifying details on the internet? You potentially have the motivation and focus required to give your writing strong arguments. Not everyone finds researching fun, so good research skills can be hard to develop. However, since schoolwork often relies on it, having a prior interest in research will give you an edge!

Solid Understanding of the Topic vs. Misused Jargon or Information

Sometimes you love a topic so much you've researched it already in your spare time. Since you know it inside and out, writing about it feels like second nature to you. That is an excellent strength for blog writers who need to find their niche—topics they know AND care about. Whenever you're allowed to choose something to write about, make sure to lean into your knowledge base. Write about something familiar. This will make the writing process even easier.

Concise Writing vs. Unnecessary Additions

Not all writing projects involve huge word counts. Sometimes the real challenge is getting a good idea into a thousand words or less. It might be tempting to leave out details or skip to the good part, but with concise writing skills, you can maximize sentence structure and the use of specific words to get your point across. Find yourself reordering sentences or using a thesaurus thoughtfully? What about pre-planning your paper in detail? If so, you're likely ready to hone your writing for maximum efficiency!

Vivid Verbs and Adjectives vs. Boring Writing

Did you know that non-fiction writing also requires strong specific verbs and adjectives? You might think that novels and poetry need to be descriptive and flowy. Yet, non-fiction projects, like essays, suffer when you fail to incorporate active verbs or detail-focused adjectives. Non-fiction can become dry rather quickly without some power and spice added. However, as you pursue power in your writing, make sure to use a thesaurus carefully, understanding the different connotations of the words provided.

Focused Sentences vs. Long-winded Sentence Structure

When you start writing for your teacher, you might find yourself trying to use words in an elevated kind of way. You want to sound smart, right? However, when attempting to show we know the material, we can inadvertently talk around the subject. If you can appreciate straightforward sentence structure, you're more likely to avoid run-ons and unnecessary word usage. Maximize your sentences for a concise and polished project.

Flowing Structure vs. Jarring Transitions

How do you go about describing a person? Do you jump from the head to the hands to the shoes and then back up to the shoulders? Or would it make more sense to move in a single direction, from head to toe or vice versa? Understanding how to arrange information will result in clearer explanations and skillful writing. Find yourself planning how and when to share facts and details? You might already know how to create a logical flow. With the proper use of transition words, like' however' and' therefore,' your audience will read the flowing structure smoothly.

Well-used Rhythm vs. Zero Rhythm

After finishing a paragraph, do you enjoy sitting down and reading it aloud to yourself? As you read, do you notice hiccups in the flow and disruption in pacing? Writers who sense rhythm recognize the power of transition words while understanding the balance between long and short sentences. They know where shorter ones, as well as punctuation, can provide natural pauses. As a result, your writing will sound great whether read aloud or silently, appealing to the inner voice inside our heads.

Great Understanding of Grammar vs. Poor Use of Grammar

The final steps of the writing process, editing, and proofreading aren't always easy. However, understanding grammar and an eye for detail will make the polishing phase a piece of cake. Not only will recognizing strong sentence structure be helpful, but a solid understanding of grammar will improve the overall quality of your writing. As a result, even if your ideas aren't super original or groundbreaking, the reading experience will be easier and more enjoyable.

The Power of Critical Thinking

Now that you understand the importance of knowing yourself and your strengths, you might want to get started on analyzing your abilities. Before you do, however, it's important to note that assessing your skills with critical thinking doesn't mean encouraging negative thinking or discouraging self-talk. In actuality, it is a way to use reasoning, communication, and experience to look at yourself and impartially analyze evidence of your abilities. It's easy to look down on yourself when you don't apply critical thinking to the challenges ahead of you.

Instead of focusing on past failures or current weaknesses, what are your strengths? What can you bring to the table? It's OK to slow down. Give yourself time to take stock of your abilities and prepare for the road ahead. Once you understand what you can achieve, you'll be more ready for the journey to powerful writing than you first thought!

In Summary

Top Tip: Get To Know Yourself!

Knowing yourself requires sitting down and thinking about your experiences. It might not feel great at first, but you can start analyzing yourself objectively as a writer by using the writing checklist below. After all, the "you of today" cannot define the potential of the future!

CHALLENGE!

It's time to sit down and consider your strengths as a writer. Choose at least three skills that already feel comfortable. Which of the following can you check off?

- innovative concepts
- concise writing
- vivid verbs and adjectives
- strong research abilities
- focused sentences
- flowing transitions
- solid understanding of the topic
- well-used rhythm

Next, consider the boxes you didn't check off. These may be areas you have to work on as a writer. Choose one skill to start working on today! Finally, keep an eye out for it as you go through this book, so you can start practising it as soon as possible.

Snapshot

It's easy to feel overwhelmed when faced with a blank page, and you may be struggling with a lack of inspiration or motivation. Use self-awareness and critical thinking skills to assess your strengths and weaknesses. Once you figure out whether you're good at thinking up ideas, writing well, or editing carefully, you'll have a better idea of where you can improve. Common obstacles to a polished work include— vague ideas, misinformation, bad sentence structure, fluff, and poor editing. That doesn't have to stop you, though! As you work through the rest of this book, you can keep your strengths and weaknesses in mind and target the specific writing goal you want to achieve.

Chapter 2
What Are Study Skills and How Do I Create Them?

Now that you know your writing strengths and weaknesses, you probably feel like you have a better idea of what to do next, right? Sitting down at your desk, you look at all the reading you need to get done, open up a blank document, and... now what? Should you start writing an outline or research? What needs to get done first, and what exactly does your project require? Can you keep focused on your work when your family is making a lot of noise in the next room?

Knowing your strengths and weaknesses is only half the battle. It's time to provide another set of firm foundations that will help you achieve success in writing. Before you start, however, you need to think about your study skills, habits, environment, and plan. If you understand how to study and maximize your time well, you'll be empowered to form healthy study habits and a more focused action plan. On top of that, with the best study environment created to suit your particular needs, you're more likely to set your plans in motion. But how do you make sure that you'll succeed? It's time to take a closer look at these essential foundations for the best studying practices!

What Are Study Skills?

One of the most important skill sets you'll need to get under your belt is study skills. These are techniques and approaches to study that can often be applied to many other life skills, including finishing jobs at work or getting housework done. Whether you're working with people or not, you must rely on a variety of communication tools and techniques to achieve your goals. Furthermore, you'll have to understand how to manage and take care of yourself, making sure that you take breaks, learn from mistakes, and maintain motivation. Some of these skills may already be familiar to you, which should make this process a little easier, but perhaps there are a few things you haven't considered.

Working With People

Whether you're a professional working with a team or a student trying to get a group project done, communication with others is a key part to study skills. Even if you're working alone on a report or essay, you have to take the person who will be reading your writing into account. Understanding how to work with others is a vital part of study skills and, when properly handled, will be a crucial foundation for success.

Capitalizing on Teamwork

What if you struggle to understand an idea or where to start a project? Don't let yourself get lost in your work. Instead, reach out to friends or fellow students and ask for their input. If possible, speak with your professor or teacher to get a better perspective of the project. Sometimes feedback can be discouraging, and if your friends are as lost as you are, this can be misleading. But learning to work with others can be a great study skill that applies to all areas of life, including family, relationships, and work environments.

Negotiating and Persuading

Many times when you're writing an essay, especially higher-level academic ones, you may be asked to prove a point. Blog posts with marketing aims are also invested in persuading the reader to invest in a brand or consider the advice and products you're offering. Whatever the situation, learning how to negotiate and persuade using a skillful blend of facts and strong communication skills can also help you out in your career and professional life, as well as your writing.

Communicating Clearly

It can be hard to be open and honest about your vision, ideas, or feelings on a topic, but understanding how to communicate clearly and respectfully is an important study skill. Teamwork should become smoother when you have a concise and straightforward ability to communicate through speaking and writing. Your teacher will recognize that you understand the material you're discussing. On top of that, clear communication will empower your readers to learn and take action, which is particularly important for bloggers.

Knowing and Targeting Your Audience

Negotiation and open communication are usually easier if you know who you're writing for well. Think about who you're trying to communicate with. Are they a younger sibling, your mom or dad, your teacher, your boss, professor, or a target audience online? Depending on who they are, you're going to share your ideas or information differently, right? For example, some professors prefer tons of sources and lots of facts, whereas other instructors want to see a more laid-back approach to writing. Some audiences appreciate more formality and data, and others are more likely to enjoy conversational writing styles with easy-to-digest information. Whoever is reading your writing or listening to you speak should determine how you approach communication.

Giving and Receiving Constructive Feedback

After working hard on a project or blog post, receiving constructive feedback can be difficult. However, if your goal is to reach a target audience or get a good mark on a project, you have to be ready to accept the fact that something may have slipped past your notice. Whether positive or negative, accepting constructive feedback is a crucial study skill, especially at work or in school. At the same time, giving constructive feedback can be equally challenging. You might be wondering, "How do I share my concerns about the project?" or, "This feels wrong, but I'm not sure." In either case, be honest about your viewpoint and limitations. It's important because it allows you to help your fellow students on their path to academic or professional achievement. It's an excellent way for you to practice your study skills and practically use your knowledge.

Achieving Your Goals

Beyond working with people, study skills also include understanding the practicalities behind achieving your goals. What are you trying to learn or do? How are you going to organize the data at your fingertips? Where are you going to look for information? How will you make this information relevant for your audience? All of these questions point to the importance of using study skills while researching, organizing information, and writing. Many of these skills require a lot of reading and understanding of how to handle information. Let's take a closer look!

Understanding Complex Texts

It doesn't matter whether you are a young writer or a mature student. You will always find yourself facing a new challenge, academic or professional. This means that you might be faced with complex texts, reports, books, or novels to read as the basis for your studies. For some of us, reading is second nature. Give us a good book or essay, and we will be happy to figure out the meaning and ideas. For others, reading through academic papers or thick novels might feel overwhelming. However, learning how to read well, scan for general ideas, and skim for other details, is a study skill that must be developed over time. With this foundational skill set, research, problem-solving, and practically applying solutions will come more naturally.

Using Computers and Technology Thoughtfully

You probably already know that navigating the internet is not as easy as it looks. Not all websites provide accurate research, and many scholarly papers require special permissions or payment to access. Even when searching Google, it's important to understand how to use the search engine well. With practice, you will know how to use appropriate keywords and pick trustworthy websites to locate the research information you seek to find. Be careful, though. Writers at the top of the Google search page may not necessarily be as reliable as you would hope. Some may be manipulating Google's algorithm with special writing techniques. That is why it is important to first look for information from books at the library before accessing other sources online.

Managing Information and Research Well

While reading through your research, you might find yourself maximizing time and energy by making notes, using sticky notes, or photocopying/printing pages for future use. One of the best ways to manage your research is to start a citation list. There are quite a few online websites that help you reference your information sources easily. An example is myBib, which creates a Reference page for you. Taking notes as you read along is highly recommended, as well as directly inputting the data you discover into your outline with the in-text citations. This way, you don't have to retrace your steps online or in the library.

Save time by keeping those library and website visits to a minimum!

Organizing Information

As mentioned above, you can organize your information by using bookmarks (for online websites), online reference collators, sticky notes, or lists. Taking notes on paper or sticky notes is highly recommended because the act of writing often reinforces the knowledge you're processing. Later, I will share with you the importance of drafting outlines. Directly inputting information into your outline, with clear in-text citations, won't only help you retrace your steps if you need information, but it will also give you an idea of where your writing is less supported than others. For less academic writers, organizing information may be as simple as understanding what logical progression you need to follow to draw your reader in and inform them.

Seeing the "Big Picture"

Gathering tons of information, a less well-known study skill, involves the ability to understand the "big picture." What does this project have to do with the rest of the course? Why is my teacher giving me this project? What am I supposed to learn from this? These are a few questions that you can ask yourself as a way to understand what direction you want to pursue in your investigation. The ability to synthesize and bring together what you learn is a study skill that can be applied in many areas, including contextualizing professional work or navigating relationships.

Using Creativity and Innovation

Imagine how your teacher or reader feels. Sitting down to read through a stack of essays or browsing through clickbait might be an extremely frustrating experience. That is why when you sit down to plan what you are going to write; you need to think of ways to bring creativity and innovation to your essay or article. How can you make your project more interesting and engaging? If you understand your audience well, you will also know how to bring them information in a fresh way that will keep their interest. Not only will you be capturing their attention, but you'll also be giving yourself creative inspiration and motivation during the study phase of your project.

Noticing Patterns, Connections, Trends, and Details

Another essential skill tied to studying and writing involves the ability to make connections, follow trends, notice small details, and then draw a pattern out of them. If you can recognize patterns and relationships between data, you'll be able to organize the information in your writing in a creative yet concise way, as well as 'wow' your audience with potentially new perspectives they hadn't considered. This ability, tied closely to seeing the "big picture," will help you draw conclusions other people might not have otherwise thought about. As a result, your writing will get your audience excited and eager to read more—exactly what you wanted!

Debating with Details, Information, and Facts

Relying on facts, logical progression, and solid research, you may need to use argumentation and debate to pose a response to a challenge, question, or problem. This doesn't mean that you're laughing at or making fun of your reader; rather, this is a way to share your ideas clearly and concisely. You can present your perspective using facts, detail, and reliable information while also addressing questions people might think about as they read along. It is important to understand various logical fallacies that you can use or misuse, such as the slippery slope fallacy or the strawman fallacy. If you hope to persuade with your writing, be careful to rely on more than charisma and word use! When applied to other areas of your life, this study skill will empower you when it comes to negotiation, communication, and compromise.

Problem Solving

Whether you're writing a blog post for your target audience or answering an essay question for an assignment, it's necessary to understand the challenge before you and figure out the steps to resolve it. As a result, problem-solving is an important study skill that you can apply to all areas of your life. Do you have a communication problem at work? Are you trying to share your feelings on a topic with a friend? Has a medical problem popped up in your life? All of these situations will require you to consider the obstacle or challenge and then figure out the steps needed to take to overcome it. If you're able to see the "big picture," notice the connections between data points, or organize the information you have, you will be better able to solve the problem you or your readers face.

Recognizing Practical Applications

Part of problem-solving involves applying practical applications where appropriate. This applies to anyone trying to write a cover letter, a blog post, or a report. Many of these writing projects benefit from dedicating a section to "now what?" You may have noticed a trend in the niche space that you write for, and you can draw connections and tease out a discovery or perspective for your readers... but now what? With a call to action or a personal or practical application carefully explored at the end, you will be able to leave your reader with a sense of energy and motivation. However, that does require that you're able to consider the impact of your findings and how they may affect your life or your readers' lives.

Managing Yourself

Now that you understand how study skills are linked to working with others and achieving your personal or academic goals, let's look at the study skills that are best applied to yourself. After all, there are things that you can train yourself in, allowing you to feel more ready and motivated for the journey ahead. Simply knowing your goals is not enough. You will have to be prepared to work on your own, learn from your mistakes, and take care of yourself along the way.

Setting and Achieving Goals

Where do you want to go? What are you aiming for? It's easy to dismiss these questions. You probably already have an idea of what you want, but I encourage you to sit down and write a detailed list of what you want to achieve. This doesn't just have to apply to your writing goals, but also your general studies, career, or even personal life. Something as simple as "getting an A on this essay assignment" is a good start. Understanding that goal, you can pull out your teacher's rubric (or ask them for one) so that you know what exactly you need to achieve to get an A. Having figured out your goal, you are now poised with a single focus that you can aim toward, and with the other study skills below, you can maintain your momentum to achieve the goal.

Recognizing and Maintaining Motivation

Part of the challenge when you're working on your own or handling a self-imposed task is maintaining motivation. What is going to keep you going until the end? Setting and achieving goals is an integral part of creating energy and inspiration. However, other methods can also help you maintain motivation over long periods. It doesn't matter whether you are trying to write a 10-page paper, cleaning your room, or going shopping. If you are struggling to stay on task, you can use practical study habits to keep yourself motivated to achieve the goal you set for yourself. Below, we will go into some very simple study habits you can start today!

Learning from Your Mistakes

Who enjoys failure? No one. It can be hard to process the mistakes you made, especially after working so hard on something. During these moments, it's OK to step away for a day in order to get a better perspective. The ability to step away and then return to consider your mistakes is a study skill that can impact other areas of your life, such as resolving conflict or handling challenges in the workplace. When it comes to writing, specifically, take the time to think about the writing process you just experienced and how you could improve on it the next time. Should you have done more research? Could your outline have been more focused? Were your word choices lacking? Whatever the case is, don't beat yourself up! Instead, remind yourself that you're on a journey to excellence, and this is just another step to success.

Taking Care of Yourself

In the course of a work or school project, procrastination, disorganization, and poor time management can cause you to feel the deadline crunch. You might not have enough time to eat and sleep properly, pushing yourself up to the morning of the deadline. At the last minute, you might find yourself running around, feeling more confused and tense because of last-minute problems that have cropped up. In these moments, it's essential to draw on a rarely mentioned life skill that plays a significant role in study as well —take care of yourself! This means that you should plan breaks, snacks, meals, and sleep into your schedule. We'll take a closer look at this later on, but it's something to keep in mind!

Staying Calm and Hanging in There

Even if you're well-organized, got all your study habits down, and take care of yourself, you still might feel stressed out about the project before you. Whether you are worried about your thesis or starting a new niche for your blog, it's important to trust in yourself and the preparations that you made. Give yourself some space to breathe, and remember to give yourself a little pep talk. It can be hard to regulate your emotions. However, with self-affirmation or meditation exercises, as well as appropriate breaks, you can keep yourself feeling empowered and confident, whatever task you have to handle. With all this preparation under your belt, you've got this!

What Are Study Habits?

Now that you understand what study skills you can develop over time, you might have a better idea of what kind of study habits you wish to encourage as you build your writing skills. Study habits are very practical steps that you can take to support your study skills. They will not only help you survive your writing challenge but also thrive! Here are a few study habits that you might want to consider!

- Set up a study plan that keeps your daily life requirements in mind.
- Create a good study environment for yourself to focus in.
- Keep your routine consistent while allowing for emergencies.
- Give yourself time for rest, snacks, and short breaks.
- Tackle the most complex parts of the project first.
- Review your notes regularly.

What study habits are you going to develop? That will depend on what habits you have already formed. Perhaps in the list mentioned, you already have an idea of what you need to work on next. Whatever the case, creating healthy study habits will empower you to make the most of your time, energy, and ideas so that you won't lose inspiration or motivation.

Creating the Perfect Studying Environment

As mentioned above, finding the right studying environment for your studies and writing is an essential factor in success. When you understand yourself, and what you need for academic or professional motivation, you will know what kind of environment will suit you best. There are a few ways to consider study spaces, such as do you want to decrease distractions, increase inspiration, encourage energy, or achieve comfort?

If you're looking to decrease distractions, the obvious choice would be a quiet place, removed from others and excessive noise. These study environments may include a private office, a study nook in your library's silent study zone, or your bedroom. If you choose to listen to music, you will want to vibe on ambient or nature sounds that are quieter and more chill. You can choose settings on your phone apps to temporarily silence your notifications, as well as minimize the headings and information on your writing software to give you a pure blank canvas to work with.

For those who want to increase inspiration, changing up your work locale might give you the motivation you need. Try changing your study environment by visiting a local coffee shop or park. Many of these places will have good lighting and hopefully a great view that you can take in while you are thinking through your work. Chill music with a nice upbeat that inspires you is a great backdrop for this study space. However, try to keep your phone or tablet notifications off so that you can use them without getting distracted by social media.

What about encouraging energy? Some days, I just don't feel like working. Maybe you struggle with that as well. You will discover that places like coffee shops, parks, or even your kitchen are great environments since they are often filled with sound and the energy of other people. Still, you will need to bring along some headphones, if only as a signal to not be interrupted. What if you don't have access to these alternatives? You can always put on some upbeat, energetic music or coffee-shop-ambiance sound mixes that will liven the atmosphere of your study space. Set up an app or alarm system on your phone that gives you five-minute breaks every twenty minutes. This way, you can focus on completing your goal in achievable spurts that will also keep you energized.

Some of us need a comfy, relaxing space to work in. Whether you're an older student or someone with specific physical needs, you might be looking for a physically relaxing study environment. In this case, try to choose rooms with good natural lighting and comfortable seating. Avoid areas that have loud, sudden noises or hard seating, and try to choose a location that allows you to go for short walks or a breath of fresh air. If you are particularly sensitive to temperatures, you will want to ensure that you aren't too close to an air conditioner or heating vent. With a carefully chosen study space, you will be able to focus on your work without exacerbating any physical conditions that you may be struggling with.

What if you can't choose your study environment? Unfortunately, you might not be able to choose a specific place to study in. Perhaps your only option is your bedroom. Whatever the case may be, consider all of the tips above to make your space as personalized as possible, supporting your writing and academic needs as necessary. This might mean that you will have to change up your bedroom curtains, crack open a window, put on some music, or reorganize your living room layout. Still, considering that your academic or professional success is at stake, recognizing your study environment needs and addressing them is incredibly important.

In Summary

Top Tip: Make Time To Take Breaks!

You just want to get this essay, blog post, or email

done. I get that. We've all been there, yet it's essential to keep in mind the value of preparation, self-care, and patience. Make sure that you're setting time aside for breaks, snacks, and a breath of fresh air; otherwise, you'll find yourself running out of energy and motivation in the long run.

CHALLENGE!

Do you have good study habits and a helpful study environment? Perhaps you already feel ready. But if you're wondering how to improve your approach to writing and studying, consider the following checklists and questions;

My Study Habits:

- Am I struggling with following my current study plan? If yes, do I have a good study plan? How can I improve it?
- Is my study environment supporting my specific study needs?
- How am I keeping myself motivated and consistent?
- Which part of the project should I focus on first?

- Is reviewing my notes easy? If not, in what way can I improve my note-taking?

My Study Environment:

- What kind of study environment do I need?
- What alternative places for study do I have available?
- Does my study space have easy access to rest areas, natural light, and fresh air?

Snapshot

Like many life skills, study skills can provide you with alternative approaches to everyday problems. Whether you are working in a team, assessing and achieving your goals, or taking care of yourself, study skills will ease the process of learning, including writing. Beyond developing these abilities, it's good to form healthy study habits and create a supportive study environment.

Chapter 3
Forming a Study Plan

Keeping the study skills you want to develop in mind, as well as understanding what study habits you want to pursue and what kind of study environment you need, it's time to formulate a study plan! Follow these simple steps to create a study plan tailored for you.

First - Know Your Goals

Using the study skills above, evaluate your academic and writing goals. It doesn't matter if you are trying to add new content to your social media platform or are completing an essay for a school assignment. There are a few questions that you need to answer in detail.

- What are you trying to accomplish?
- What do you want your final project to look like?
- What is your project about?
- What will you have to research and explain?
- What study skills will you need to use?
- What study skills do you want to develop?
- What study environment will boost my productivity?

If you can specify the goals that you're aiming toward, you'll be better positioned to maximize your time, energy, and environment. Once you understand what direction you hope to head in, it's time to consider what time management obstacles are standing in your way.

Second - Assess Your Current Schedule

We all have lives beyond our work and school, so keeping our daily schedules in mind during our planning phase is essential. Do you have family obligations, chores, or other jobs on the side that you are juggling? Has your boss given you multiple projects to handle? What time has been set aside for entertainment, food, and sleep? Keeping all of this balanced might be difficult, but there are ways to get a handle on the crazy timeline we call life.

- Sit down with a pen and a piece of paper and draw a sketch outline of your weekly or biweekly cycle.
- Take into consideration your sleep cycle and biological clock.
- Make sure you have set enough time aside to allow for healthy eating, exercise, and entertainment.

If you make time to assess your current life schedule and consider upcoming events and weekly tasks, you'll have a much better idea of when you can set time aside to focus on writing. An honest and accurate understanding of your life, both its needs and responsibilities, is a crucial step to creating a consistent writing routine.

Third - Plan a Consistent Study Routine

Once you have a better idea of what you need to thrive on, you can look closer at your schedule, make room for the necessary life activities, and then set time aside for your writing and studying. Make sure that some of your study periods fall during high-energy hours so that you aren't approaching writing with little to no power for motivation.

- Use your current schedule assessment to plan an achievable study routine.
- Use a productivity app to ensure that tasks, deadlines, and routine self-care are tracked clearly.
- Try to choose a free time for writing and study during a time of day when you have more physical and mental energy.

With the road laid out before you, you're on the right track to professional and academic success. By creating a personalized schedule that plays to your strengths, you are much more likely to maintain motivation and keep your routines consistent, leading to higher chances of success.

Fourth - Take Emergencies Into Account

Before setting it in stone, it's a good idea to double-check your schedule, keeping potential emergencies in mind. This is particularly important for long-term planning if you are trying to create a schedule that will last a few months or longer. You might want to consider emergencies, like illness or social gatherings. These can often derail your planned night for writing or study, so make sure you create backup plans!

- When scheduling for a specific assignment, set the deadline three days beforehand to give yourself a buffer.
- Don't allow small, 'insignificant' tasks to pile up the day before the deadline.
- Plan backup times that you can use for study and writing if something derails your study time.

It's all too easy to find yourself running out of time at the last minute. Something as simple as printing off an essay or finding a stapler can cause a ton of stress if you don't give yourself a buffer for emergencies. While it's OK to hope for the best, allowing time for mistakes and emergencies will improve your study experience overall.

Finally, Revisit Your Schedule

After two weeks of sticking to your new study and work schedule, it's a good idea to revisit your schedule and think about how it is or isn't working for you. If changes need to be made, it's a good idea to alter the study schedule too. Sometimes what you think is doable just doesn't work out, or perhaps a more severe long-term life change has suddenly popped up. Ask yourself some of these questions to get you started:

- Am I getting enough breaks, food, and sleep?
- Over the past few weeks, what have my stress levels been like?
- Do I feel like I'm getting somewhere in terms of my goals?
- Have I achieved the goals I set for myself in each section? If not, why not?
- Is there anything I should change?

When we plan for our goals, often, our predictions aren't as detailed as they could be. We don't take into account simple, everyday distractions and obstacles, like traffic, bus delays, or phone calls from family. It's impossible to plan for everything that could happen, but after trying out your schedule for a week or two, you can always revisit your study plans and tweak them as necessary. Before you know it, you will be achieving major milestones!

In Summary

Top Tip: Try out the Stream Of Consciousness Method!

This method of outlining involves having a vague starting point and jotting down every thought that comes to mind that you could potentially write about. If creating rigid plans isn't your thing, stream of consciousness allows you to start with general ideas and narrow them down throughout the writing process. This method is particularly useful for fictional pieces.

Challenge!

Consider the following questions to evaluate whether you have a solid study plan that is practical for the writing task you face. By creating a plan that has a clear structure, you'll be more likely to stick to it and achieve your goals.

- What are my goals?
- How can I achieve my goals? What exact steps should I take?
- What kind of schedule does my life have right now?
- How can I fit in studying and writing?
- What are my backup plans if my study plans are disrupted?
- Have I given myself room for disruptions?
- Is the schedule I planned for myself working out for me?

Snapshot

It's time to reflect on your journey so far. Now that you have taken your study skills, habits, and environment into account, look around you. How has your study space changed? What new perspective do you have on your goals and needs? Do you have a better idea of how to break down your assignment into smaller, achievable steps? Will you be able to maintain your new, personalized schedule long-term? After taking stock, it's time to take a deep breath and congratulate yourself on how far you've come. So far, it might feel like you're just standing around, over-thinking your problems. But half of the battle is knowing yourself and understanding what direction you need to head.

Chapter 4
Additional Tips for Students With Other Needs

As a teacher or parent, you might already feel very familiar with creating study plans, developing healthy study habits, and creating a helpful study environment. However, some students and beginner writers may require additional support as they pursue their personal, academic, and professional goals. You, yourself, your student, or your child may be juggling special academic needs alongside the usual study challenges. Many of the tips and techniques mentioned in the previous chapters can still be applied, but some need to be reiterated or supplemented depending on the specific needs of your students.

Dyslexia and Dysgraphia

Language-based learning disabilities like dyslexia, and dysgraphia, can make reading and writing much harder. Students diagnosed with these specific learning disabilities may require special support, like school or campus study skills groups or note-taking services. As a teacher or parent, you may be able to help your student and budding writer by reading the material aloud for them or giving them a reading buddy to process any research. Phonetic dictionaries and the use of specialized fonts (available for digital texts) can also help aid in research, and reading, while rewriting or copying a fellow student's notes can help cement knowledge.

For adult writers and students with dyslexia, there are many tools that can make studying, research, and writing easier. Dictation software is another helpful aid in getting words onto paper. However, once you have your paragraph set, you should make sure to read it aloud or record it onto your smartphone. If you have a friend or family member who is willing to listen, read your paper aloud to them. By listening to yourself or getting feedback from your audience, you can make notes on what needs to be changed.

ADHD

Although raising awareness about ADHD has provided students with the support they require, it is all too common to feel discouraged about the perceived limitations of being a student with this disorder. However, teachers and parents can rely on a variety of study approaches that will give their students and children solid academic support. For example, rethinking how education can happen is a great start. Take reading, for starters. Many of us know that reading is largely a passive activity. It doesn't have to be that way, though. With active reading skills developed, your student or child can engage with the text through underlining, highlighting, writing in margins, or reading aloud. Sometimes, rewriting notes or pieces of the text, talking about what they just read, or even doodling while listening to an audiobook can help them stay focused on the topic they are researching. Many experts recommend giving your student or child a sugary fruit drink, which they can sip slowly for a brain boost.

Adult learners with ADHD can overcome many distractions through the regular practice of healthy study habits. However, even if you give yourself

How to Write a Paragraph Using Study Skills

longer periods of time for study, frequent breaks, and a distraction-free environment, you might feel like you still struggle to remain focused while studying. Other specific techniques can help you keep motivated and focused. For example, creating flashcards or practice tests can help you remain invested in your studies since you're not passively processing data. The SQ4R method can also be a helpful approach to studying when you have to read heavy texts.

- S = Survey. This means that you look over the main headings and get a general feel for what you are reading.
- Q = Question. After reading the main headings, write down a list of questions for which you want to find answers.
- 4R = Read, (w)Rite, Recite, and Review. This part of the reading process involves four more steps. Read through small sections at a time. As you finish each part, write down any answers to your questions that pop up. Recite the information out loud. Then, review your questions and their answers.

Learning by rote is not always the path to a great education. Instead, it is better to invest your time in learning how to make the information your own, how to explain it in your own words, and how to practically apply it to your studies or life. When you focus on the life and study skills you need, taking the time to make them your own, you will rediscover the motivation you need to achieve the goals you have set for yourself.

Autism Spectrum Disorder

For those who have to contend with an aspect of Autism Spectrum Disorder, academic success can become much more complicated. Many study skills that others take for granted will not come easily to you. As mentioned before, however, the main thing to keep in mind is giving yourself more time to process the information before you and to remain organized. Are you hyper-organized or super disorganized? Once you figure this out, you can start with the small yet important steps of organization and preparation. Either way, you'll want to make sure that your study environment has as few sensory distractions as possible. On top of that, it's a good idea to really focus on time management, breaking your goal into smaller achievable goals. Finding a supportive study partner or encouraging friend may also help you keep focused and make sure that you take care of yourself during the study process.

When your child or student struggles with academic achievement because they're on the autistic spectrum, it can be hard to figure out what to do to be the most effective supporter. For teachers and parents especially, using short sentences to explain the material or information will help a lot. Verbally working through what was learned will help your student/child out. There are other practical steps you can take to ease the journey to academic success.

- Provide a stress ball or playdough.
- Set up an easy to manage day planner to help study sessions, breaks, and other events in your life.
- Use an accordion file to hold loose papers and notes.
- Calculate what is most important to focus on. Don't waste time on an 8% weighted project!
- Ask questions when needed.

Asking questions all the time can get difficult. Still, if you need to double-check the meaning of what someone says in class, you should feel free to discuss it with a fellow student or your teacher. Find someone you can talk to about the concepts you're learning so that you can process the information in another way, making it your own and visualizing it more clearly.

Special Needs

In a world that often determines a person's value by their academic success, it can be hard to remember that life skills are more essential to learn than academic ones. Attitude and character-building provide long-term support, allowing your child to overcome obstacles in the future, even when you're absent. What do you want your child to learn? Consider some of these traits that may create an independent and motivated mind within your child, regardless of their academic skills:

- self-awareness
- self-confidence
- perseverance
- agency
- goal-setting
- stress management
- receiving and giving help

How to Write a Paragraph Using Study Skills

When your child or student struggles with studying (and writing) thanks to special needs and other disabilities, you'll be faced with another level of challenge—figuring out what their needs are and how you can provide for them. Observing and focusing on your child/student will allow you to recognize their particular strengths and weaknesses. When you understand where they require support, you'll be better able to advocate for them. On top of that, you'll understand what behavior and learning strategies you must model for them to follow.

For parents, getting involved with their child's school is a crucial step. It not only signals to the staff that your child's future matters to you, but it will also help you understand how to continue the learning process at home. Discuss with your child's teacher what kind of learning type your child might be. Are they visual, auditory, or kinesthetic learners? Recognizing these differences will allow you to teach essential life skills to your child at home in a way that they can understand. Overall, remember that your child's learning disability doesn't have to destroy their chance for happiness and personal success.

Snapshot

With your goals and plans clearly defined, you are ready to take on the writing process! In the following chapters, we'll be looking at five simple steps to writing a powerful paragraph, starting with understanding what role a paragraph plays in any written work. From there, you'll explore the different types of paragraphs, what makes a good paragraph, and the editing process. All these phases of writing rely on the study skills we discussed in previous chapters, so you can say that you've already solved half of the problem. Now, let's get you writing some powerful paragraphs! With these goals in mind, you can formulate a personalized study plan that will provide you with the academic or professional help you need. However, when other learning disabilities or special needs are a factor, additional strategies may have to be used to achieve your goals.

Chapter 5
Step 1: Understanding the Functions and Purpose of a Paragraph

Have you ever seen pictures of the Leaning Tower of Pisa? Did it get you thinking about what it would be like to live in a crooked house? Stories exist of homes that collapsed due to crookedly aligned walls or the use of poorly-made building materials. Hence when building homes, understanding how to form solid bricks and align them well will determine how long your walls stay standing.

Sitting down to write an assignment is no different. Blog posts, essays, novels, and personal statements all have one thing in common. They're composed of smaller units known as paragraphs. Think of these as the bricks that make up a wall. Without forming them properly and aligning them carefully with each other, your wall is sure to look crooked or even fall. In the same way, before you sit down to write, you should know what a paragraph is and how they're laid out, depending on the purpose of your overall project.

What Is a Paragraph?

You may already know what a paragraph is, but let's revisit the basic definition as a refresher. Paragraphs contain sentences related to each other, which address a single topic. Well-written paragraphs get organized logically, focus on one idea, and use varied sentence structures to keep things fresh.

More often than not, paragraphs, when combined, provide multiple perspectives or details on a larger, more general topic or argument. For example, you might be writing a blog post about owning a car for the first time. One paragraph may deal with general car care, another with seasonal, and a final might touch on the importance of knowing your car's specific upkeep requirements. Overall, each paragraph should stick to a single topic with the necessary details, information, and support statements following the topic sentence. In addition, when integrating paragraphs, transition sentences are needed to encourage flow. Envision paragraphs as having the general structure below you can utilize for any writing project:

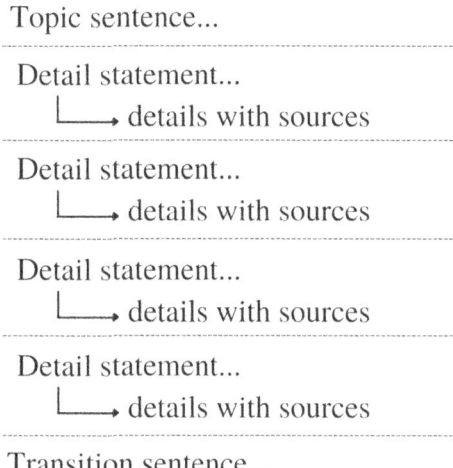

Already you might have noticed that paragraph organization is tied to its general-purpose—communication. Think about all the times you have hung out and chatted with friends and family. When we talk with people, we might notice that some tend to wander from the topic while others might struggle to give you all of the details you need. These kinds of issues in communication can make the passing of information difficult.

That is why, when it comes to writing, you have a chance to arrange your thoughts. Stick to the topic at hand through the use of well-organized paragraphs and use them to describe, narrate, discuss, or persuade. The goal is to communicate your ideas effectively in a focused, clearly defined way.

Remember, combine your paragraphs with well-crafted transitions to create a harmonious whole, sure to catch your reader's eye!

Paragraphs... What's the Big Deal?

After understanding what a paragraph is and how it's built, you might be thinking, "So what? What's the big deal with paragraphs?" Well, for starters, they're a way to make written communication effective. If we follow the formula shown above, we can easily comprehend ideas and information in all kinds of situations.

Of course, the first thing you might be thinking about is school assignments. If you attended grade school, high school, or college, you probably remember the stress of writing a book report, essay, or science report. All of these writing projects require you to use paragraphs. If you are planning to pursue further academic study or academic work, the prospect of writing for journals and other publications might be looming on the horizon. As such, paragraphs will be a big part of your future.

But what about professional life? Apart from the more practical, hands-on professions, many careers require basic knowledge of communication. You might use paragraphs to write a cover letter for a new job, head up a marketing campaign, or compose blog posts for your business's social media platforms. Whatever the case, understanding how to organize your thoughts and leverage the power of your words in concisely formed paragraphs is a crucial part of empowered communication.

Even your personal life is not entirely free from the necessity of using thoughtful, organized writing. A simple email, personal statements, resumes, and even your diary are places where paragraphs are sure to pop up. Communicating to loved ones or yourself will become easier with practice and forethought. When you combine the writing practices outlined in the rest of the book with the study skills we reviewed earlier, your approach to writing should become more concise, easily understood, and interesting.

Since paragraphs are used in so many areas of our lives, it's essential to understand which type we should use for each situation we face. On top of that, recognizing who we are writing for can also determine the tone and form of expression we use while composing it.

General Writing Approaches to Paragraphs

After figuring out what kind of paragraphs are needed to make up the body of your writing project, it's time to consider the audience and writing style. Your audience can change from project to project, and with that comes a difference in approach, which will impact your writing style. Before setting pen to paper, it's a good idea to think about who you're writing for and what tone they're expecting. It's not simply a case of knowing what they want and giving it to them, but also understanding how to speak their language and attract them with specific writing styles. So, where do you start?

Know Your Audience

To begin with, you need to think about who is going to read your writing. One of the vital study skills mentioned earlier—is knowing your audience. Is it a teacher, a friend, or someone online? How old are they? What walks of life do they come from? Are you trying to get them to believe, buy, or experience something?

All of these questions need to be answered before you start writing. Remember, the middle-aged woman contemplating what car to buy isn't necessarily the same as the young teen boy looking for video game guides. Generational, educational, and cultural differences need to be taken into account before writing. You should always carefully consider the impact your audience will have on your chosen approach.

Writing Styles

Once you have a specific target audience in mind, it's time to think about how they communicate and process information. Should you be writing formally or informally? Should your writing approach be more conversational and narrative-driven, or should it be concise and filled with detailed data? What are the word count limits for the project? When these variables are taken into account, you'll have a better idea of how to present what you want to share.

Since your audience determines how you approach writing, it's a good idea to be concise and use a practical application of study skills. This will bring value to the table for your reader. Respect your audience's time and interest by avoiding fluff and padding. Keep in mind that some of your choices will also determine how long your sentences will be, what terms and jargon you can use, as well as what level of vocabulary. All these factors can help you define and shape the writing goal you wish to achieve and illustrate the steps you'll need to take moving forward.

Putting Effort Into Paragraphs

Even though there is a basic formula for paragraphs, as we discussed, the logic and progression will change depending on the purpose and audience you're trying to reach. This is why consideration, preparation, and organization are key study skills you need to develop for all future writing projects. The exciting news is that these skills and this approach to writing are transferable to other areas of life. With the ability to step back, think things through reasonably, and organize your thoughts, you'll discover how to better communicate ideas and feelings on many other topics. On top of that, taking the time to think about your audience is an opportunity to consider those around you. Your ability to understand who you're talking to will not only increase your communication skills but also support you on a journey to compassion and empathy for others!

In Summary

Top Tip: Embrace Confidence as a Writer!

This might sound a little crazy, especially if you're still in school or English isn't your first language, but assume the reader has much less knowledge than you. When you approach your writing with confidence, you can view it as an opportunity to show how much of an expert you are in what you're writing. This affects the tone and grammar used and how you outline and organize.

Challenge!

Before sitting down to write, consider your project and ask yourself some fundamental questions about the direction you want to take it in.

- Who is my target audience specifically?

- What kind of writing style should I be using?
- What am I trying to achieve with this writing project?
- What is the main point or idea?
- What paragraph types will help me reach my target audience and personal goals for the project?
- Where can I start researching or looking for information?

Snapshot

The paragraph, an essential building block of any writing project, is often overlooked. However, if you look closely at the various ways we communicate, we can see the importance of well-crafted paragraphs. It's important to remember that writing is designed for communication, and the role of the paragraph is to break up information into understandable chunks. As a result, each paragraph must have a separate topic with focused supportive statements, details, and facts. Other factors that impact the presentation and style of a paragraph are your goals and your audience. Who you are writing for will determine, for example, whether the writing is formal or informal.

Chapter 6
Step 2: Identifying Paragraphs and Recognizing the Structure of a Good One

From the Giza pyramids to the castles of Europe, and the simple architecture of Frank Lloyd Wright, humans have experimented with form and function when it comes to monuments, tombs, military bases, and homes. Each of these locations was created for a specific purpose, and the goals of their builders defined what materials and shape the building would become. In a sense, forming a paragraph is no different.

The reason for your writing project and the goals you have created will define the style and functions of the paragraphs you will be using. As mentioned earlier, for academic purposes, you will want to pursue a more formal style with persuasive or expository paragraphs that rely on logical organization and strong research. For more personal purposes, you may opt for simpler sentence structures and a conversational writing style for your narrative or descriptive paragraphs. Whatever the case, learning how to identify and analyze paragraphs is an important step toward understanding how to create a well-written one.

The Four Major Paragraph Types

Consider when you most often use a paragraph. Are you writing an essay, blog post, or personal statement? Does the assignment require you to debate a point or inform the reader through a report? If you're more creative, how would you go about writing descriptive or narrative paragraphs? Even if you're just emailing or building a resume, you'll have to think about ways to clearly, concisely, and logically present yourself through paragraphs. This is why you must understand the four main approaches to paragraph writing and how they can be applied practically.

Descriptive Paragraphs

'Overhead, the gray clouds hang with a gloomy air, bringing a cold north-easterly wind that nips at my nose and ears. As I more comfortably snuggle inside my thick winter coat, I glance up at the naked branches of the oak trees. It's quiet this time of year. No birds call out, and the chatter of scampering squirrels has been silenced. With the scatter of snowflakes muffling the rumble of passing cars, the entire world feels as though it has been plunged into a thick blanket. The only sound that sharply catches my ear is the crunch of my brown boots on the icy sidewalk.'

DESCRIPTIVE PARAGRAPHS MIGHT SOUND VERY familiar to you because they are everywhere. Usually, you will find them in novels and stories, but you might find yourself needing to describe something to a friend in an email. Whether they are reviewing a product or sharing an experience, bloggers will have to rely on descriptive paragraphs to create a striking visual.

When it comes to organizing descriptive paragraphs, logical flow is crucial because these paragraphs usually hold a lot of small details. For example, when describing a scene or a room, you might want to start from one side and move around to the other. You can also logically move in a slow circle around you. Sometimes, a top-down or bottom-up approach is also helpful for landscapes or people. For example, if you want to describe a friend, you start with their hair and work your way down to the shoes they're wearing. Either way, it's important to keep the direction linear so that the reader can fill in the details easily.

Writing descriptive paragraphs can be difficult for a variety of reasons. For instance, they can get boring easily, and you have to know which details to focus on. More often than not, the mood or tone that you aim for will dictate what adjectives and verbs you use. On top of that, you need to make sure that your description doesn't overstay its welcome. However, once you master the descriptive paragraph, you can give your writing projects and emails some zing.

Narrative Paragraphs

'Today may have been one of the worst mornings I've had in a long while. It started with the piece of lego I stepped on as I got out of bed. How it got there, I don't know, but by the time I managed to hobble to the bathroom, I had discovered that my alarm had somehow failed to go off. My kids had been running wild for the past hour and never thought about waking me up. I barely had time to brush my teeth, let alone get a bite of breakfast. Somehow I managed to get the kids to school on time, but when I got home, I realized that I had forgotten to take the dog out for a walk. So, there was that to deal with first. Then, of course, when I finally get to my desk, what's waiting for me? A ton of emails that need to be answered. It's only 10 A.M., and I'm already dead inside.'

Whenever you start explaining a situation, describing an event, or telling a story, you are talking about a narrative. Narrative paragraphs usually focus on a series of events or steps. You might be summarizing a novel for an essay, describing your experiences as a worker on your resume, explaining to your boss the process of teamwork for a project, or sharing an experience with your blog readers. Whatever the case, narrative paragraphs are incredibly useful for most writing projects.

As you can see in the example paragraph above, narrative paragraphs rely on linear progression, usually starting at the beginning and, well, finishing at the end. In some rare cases, a writer might want to take a risk and reverse the time order, but for most cases, narrative paragraphs require a sequential order of events. Time words, specific adverbs, and prepositions can help clarify the order and relative time of each sub-event in the story. For example, you might want to use words like' before," after,' or' during,' as well as other specific details like "an hour later" or "at 10 A.M." There's nothing worse than trying to follow a disjointed story, so practicing transitions is key.

Out of all the paragraphs you'll read about in this section, narrative paragraphs may feel the most familiar. This is because a large part of our communication involves telling people what's going on in our life. From talking about your schedule, your day so far, or explaining a story to your teacher, narrative paragraphs have a lot of uses. However, it is still important to practice organization and logical progression in order to avoid missing important details.

Expository Paragraphs

'Oliver Twist, written by Charles Dickens during the late 1830s, chronicles the adventures of a young boy in Victorian England. After his mother dies during childbirth in a poor house, Oliver is raised as an orphan by the less than charitable orphanage staff. When Oliver asks for seconds, he is ejected from the orphanage and forced to work for a cruel undertaker. Eventually, mistreatment forces him to run away to London, where he falls in with a band of pickpockets led by the manipulative Fagin, the mischievous Artful Dodger, and the dangerous Sykes. Oliver Twist's adventures eventually lead him to Mr. Brownlow and the promise of a more peaceful life. Whether Oliver manages to escape his past is something you will have to find out for yourself!'

LIKE NARRATIVE PARAGRAPHS, expository paragraphs rely on sequential logic and clear steps. This is because expository paragraphs involve explaining or teaching someone about something. Have you ever had to explain to someone how to drive a car or cook a particular meal? Have you had to explain how to achieve a certain kind of decor in your home? Does your teacher want you to explore an idea in a novel-based essay? All of these will require expository paragraphs, where you will have to define and break down ideas or processes into easily understood pieces.

Unlike descriptive or narrative paragraphs, the logic behind expository writing relies on a conceptual organization. This will require you to make connections, notice trends, or categorize different details into groups. For example, if you are writing on the topic, "what are the best video games of all time?" you might want first to split the outline into genres. You will look at the best video games of each genre and then draw conclusions from there. Or perhaps, you'll want to hone in on a specific genre but look at subcategories within that more detailed selection. Ultimately, how you organize the details and supportive information for your topic sentence will depend on the topic itself.

To a certain extent, expository paragraphs aren't that difficult to write. However, the conceptualization and organization that must happen before writing requires a lot more work than other paragraphs. That being said, sometimes people get too formal with expository and end up boring their audience. Taking some elements from descriptive paragraphs, such as strong adjectives and using active verbs, can add some necessary pep to your expository paragraphs.

Persuasive Paragraphs

'Variety is the spice of life, and travel is one great way to add some seasoning to your life's adventures. If life feels a little too bland, living in another country for a month is sure to give you a new perspective on the hidden potential and wisdom to be found in other cultures. That is particularly true when you get caught in a rut of normalcy at home, where it's difficult to shake free of unhealthy traditions or lifestyles. Traveling allows you to discover alternative ways to live your life, life goals, and skills to pursue. Settling into a new place often provides you an opportunity to start fresh, rebooting your habits and routines. On top of that, whenever you leave your home, you will discover the energy of exploration and challenge. In the process of overcoming obstacles, confidence and

inspiration will undoubtedly impact your attitude toward life.'

AT SOME POINT in your life, you have probably said something like, "I think you will like this because..." or, "this is a good idea, and here's why..." Whenever you have tried to persuade someone to do or think something, you rely on persuasion techniques that are often used in persuasive paragraphs. These paragraphs are the foundation of many argumentative essays, where you have to prove a certain perspective to your professor or teacher. Blog posts and personal statements can also hold persuasive elements. However, the power of the best persuasive paragraphs relies on reliable information formed through thorough research.

Persuasive paragraphs, like expository, require a lot of preparation beforehand. Not only do you have to know your stuff, but you also need solid, reliable evidence from accurate sources used carefully in your text. As a result, a well-planned outline for persuasive pieces is a must-have before you start writing. By outlining your arguments and support statements first, you can figure out the weaker areas and choose a more persuasive order for your paragraphs. However you decide to organize, each paragraph needs to be self-contained and focused, giving proper space to explain and support the point you're trying to make.

Using sources well, changing up the sentence structure in the paragraph, and choosing vivid words will pump up your persuasive paragraph. These writing techniques, combined with great organization and solid research, not only give your paragraphs energy but also work to persuade your audience. Persuasive paragraphs, therefore, do require a lot of work, but if your goal is a good mark or a brand follower, the effort will be worth it!

The Practical Functions of a Paragraph

In Chapter 5, we had a look at the basic structure of a good paragraph. Usually, paragraphs begin with a single topic sentence followed by three or more detail sentences. These detail sentences will include in-text citations, whether they're directly quoted or summarized. After the entire topic is covered, a conclusion or transition sentence is used to end the paragraph.

Let's pretend that you're writing about colonizing Mars. From the outset, you decide that you want to write an expository report in which you will describe Mars, discuss the obstacles to sustaining life, and then present the solutions. This follows a logical progression overall for the entire report, but for the purpose of analyzing paragraphs, you will look at the first section. In the first paragraph, you'll want to describe Mars generally and lay some foundational groundwork and knowledge. Keeping in mind issues that may need to be addressed in the later paragraphs, you can form a quick sketch of how to organize the first:

1. Topic sentence: Introduce Mars as close to Earth and holding potential for life.
2. detail sentence: Mars's weather
3. detail sentence: Mars's daily and yearly cycles
4. detail sentence: Mars's temperature
5. detail sentence: Mars's gravity
6. Transition sentence: There are obstacles to life on Mars.

Once you decide on a general outline for the paragraph, you are ready to start writing. So let's take a closer look at the individual parts of the paragraph and figure out how you can craft each sentence.

Topic Sentences

Topic sentences provide the framework for the entire paragraph. You can think of topic sentences as a map or a very general spoiler for what is to come. With the topic sentence set at the beginning, you are letting the reader know what to expect in the paragraph. From this point on, every detail sentence should refer back to, or enhance, the topic sentence in some way. At no point in time should you be distracting from or veering off the topic. Although fiction writers might enjoy leaving a paragraph ending on a cliffhanger, most paragraphs should not be too surprising, especially when it comes to nonfiction writing.

Why can't we add some extra details? Logical and ordered paragraphs that follow the guidelines of the topic sentence allow for easier skimming. Sometimes readers don't have a ton of time on their hands, so they will skim through the blog post or book, looking for the topic sentences that might hold the information they need. To facilitate this process, it is highly recommended to keep each of your paragraphs focused on one topic, which, in turn, is decided by the topic sentence.

So, how would you start to write about Mars? In your sketched outline, if you have already decided what direction you want to go in for the topic sentence, you might end up with one like this:

'Mars, the closest neighboring planet to Earth, provides a challenge for our vision of life on another planet.'

As you can see, this topic sentence, like most general paragraph topic sentences, only relays generic information. The overview of the paragraph does not include any of the details. That is the major difference between a thesis statement and a topic sentence. More often than not, thesis statements hold the significant points of the body paragraphs, showing the overview of the entire essay or assignment. As a result, they can end up being a few sentences long if the project is complex or lengthy. On the other hand, since topic sentences are more generalized, they need to get to the point within a sentence or two at most. Done crafting your topic sentence? It's time to get down to the main point of the paragraph!

Detail Sentences

If you visualize the topic, and transition, sentences as hamburger buns, you can imagine that the detail sentences are like the meat and salad of your meal. Detail sentences hold all of the information that supports your topic statement. That may include description details, ordered events, support for an argument, or referenced data, depending on what kind of paragraph you are writing. Using organization and logical study skills, it's a good idea to figure out how you're going to order your details and where you will use sources.

So, do you just start writing? With a good outline and noted sources on hand, you should be good to go. That being said, it's a good idea to keep transition words in mind to help your paragraph flow more smoothly if necessary. For simple paragraphs that explain a process, using words like 'First,' 'Second,' and 'Third,' are excellent starting points for beginner writers. However, with more formal or high-level writing projects, you will have to consider using alternative approaches to create complex sentence structures. Words like 'although' or 'furthermore' can add or explain your ideas more smoothly.

In this conversational paragraph about Mars, the details are introduced with simple transition words like "for starters," "on top of that," and 'furthermore.' Most of the sentences are shorter, intended to make reading the information easier. Note the different sentence structures used in this paragraph as well:

'For starters, since Mars lacks the dense atmosphere and weather systems we find on Earth, life on Mars would not have super exciting weather, except for its slow-moving tornados. On top of that, Mars's daily rotation is similar to Earth, coming in at 24.5 hours long, but its revolution around the Sun is longer. This results in a year that's almost double the length of Earth's year! During a Martian year, you'll experience four seasons, but they last longer. Thanks to Mars's distance from the Sun, its warmest temperatures land at 70 degrees Fahrenheit and drop to -225 degrees at its coldest. Furthermore, due to its lower mass, Mars generates less gravity than Earth which affects how much you weigh, allowing you to feel lighter as you walk around.'

You can imagine that this paragraph might have been written in a blog post or email for an everyday reader. The writer uses an exclamation mark and informal language to get their knowledge across simply.

There's also a lack of referenced material or in-text citations. So this piece of writing, although informative and accurate, would not be considered "a great reference resource" for more academic or professional purposes. Still, the data is shared smoothly and effectively. It only needs a closing or transition sentence!

Closing & Transition Sentences

As a mirror to the topic sentence, the closing sentence may wrap up the main idea of the paragraph by restating the topic sentence with a short takeaway note included. Time and again, you can add a short answer to the "So what?" your reader might be asking. After all, many readers, whether they are reading for fun or education, are seeking to take away something from the information in your paragraph. Are you introducing a character? In that case, you can end with a comment that hints at the mood or tone of that character moving forward. Perhaps you can foreshadow a future event. Are you addressing a solution to a problem? The closing sentence can present a call to action for the reader, encouraging them to try out the suggestions in the paragraph.

In this particular case, if our writing project was simply a description of Mars, a good closing sentence might look like this:

'Although Mars might sound like an exciting place to visit, thanks to its lack of atmosphere, and unwelcoming temperatures, it is still not suitable for human civilization.'

This leaves the reader with something to consider, which we hinted at in the topic sentence as well. However, if this paragraph were part of a larger essay or report, this kind of sentence would be too final for a body paragraph. On the other hand, transition sentences hint at what is coming next in the following paragraph. These sentences are difficult to craft because it's hard not to add extra details in this part of the paragraph, especially when you're transitioning to another section. Let's check out what a transition sentence for this topic could look like:

'All of this might sound exciting, but there is much to consider before Mars is ready to support a human colony.'

Since we decided that the next paragraph would address the major issues that arise from Mars's difficult environment, this transition sentence hints to the reader what is coming next. Once again, there should be no surprises following the transition sentence. The next line should be a new paragraph that deals with the issues that need to be considered before Mars can become a colony. In this way, the logical progression planned in the outline is kept clear for your reader, making it easier for them to follow your ideas and information. With clarity comes confidence and empowerment, so give your readers all the tools they need to understand and potentially follow through on what you've presented to them!

Know When To Start a New Paragraph

Still, you might be thinking, "But how do I know when to start a new paragraph?" The good news is that there's a straightforward answer. Outlines! Although it places an extra step in the writing process and requires more time, the investment is worth it. With an outline, you can assess your research and information, plus plan out how to logically lay it out. You'll be able to figure out what your primary points will be, which will, in turn, decide when and where your paragraphs will start and end. Outlines work for all forms of writing projects, but they're particularly useful for academic assignments since most academic papers require one argument or point to have its own paragraph. For personal or freelance work, however, paragraph separation can be determined by other factors.

For average blog audiences, readability on a smartphone is essential. Whether you have advertisements on your blog or not, you'll want to consider how your information looks to the reader's eye by choosing smaller chunks of text to encourage quick reading. Splitting paragraphs up to provide short breaks can be very helpful for online text especially, but it's also a good idea for certain novel genres, like young adult fiction.

In some cases, you might be trying to contrast two ideas or show different views on a single topic. Separating the viewpoints into their own paragraphs can help your reader understand the differing points. For example, if you're writing a blog post comparing two smartphones, maybe divide it into paragraphs with comparisons of each feature, detailed separately. You could also just describe one phone in one paragraph and then describe the second phone in the following paragraph. Each approach to logically separating information works for different audiences and in different situations. As a result, deciding how to separate your paragraph relies on what your audience is looking for or needs.

The Next Big Step

With a better understanding of why paragraphs exist and how they should be used, you are ready to take on your writing challenge. Whether you're planning to write a descriptive, narrative, expository, or persuasive paragraph, keep the outline reviewed in this chapter to hand. Relying on the paragraph formula will provide you with the support and direction you need for any writing project you're facing.

Before you start writing your powerful paragraph, however, think about the ways that the study skills you discovered earlier have helped you on your journey. Organization, logical thinking, making connections, and practically applying information have already played a large part in the writing process. So, let's pause and take stock of how far you have come! Below, you can take on a reading and analysis challenge to test your new knowledge and skills. A few paragraphs have been provided to test your understanding of paragraph types, styles, and potential audiences. Once you feel familiar and comfortable with the thought processes behind paragraph creation, the next chapter will take you step by step through a hands-on exercise to build your paragraph. If you feel ready, let's get on it! There's no time like the present!

In Summary

Top Tip: Know the Formula!

A single topic sentence can be followed by two or more detail sentences, which are then closed off with a closing or transition sentence. It's an easy formula to remember, but getting comfortable with this process of thinking might require some time. With practice, you will eventually be able to start tweaking how a paragraph might look and be ready to provide your specific readers with a more personalized form of communication.

Challenge!

Read the following paragraphs. Highlight or underline the topic sentence. Consider the following questions: What kinds of paragraphs are they? What audiences are they targeting? How does their writing style compliment their potential goals?

Paragraph one

'It's not that hard to make basic homemade crepes. You just need some flour, eggs, milk, water, and butter. Some people like to add a little bit of salt, but that's up to you. First, you should get out a mixing bowl. Whisk one cup of all-purpose flour and two eggs together. Then, with beaters or a whisk, slowly stir in half a cup of milk and half a cup of water. Once the mixture is smooth, mix in two tablespoons of melted butter and a pinch of salt. With the crepe mix done, warm up a frying pan with a little bit of oil or butter. I would recommend medium-high heat. I usually make one ladle for each crepe, but it really depends on the size of your frying pan. You can measure out one-quarter of the batter for each crepe if you prefer. After pouring the crepe out, tilt the pan a little in a circular motion so that the crepe covers the whole pan evenly. Wait for a couple of minutes. Usually, you can see the edges cook through first. When the bottom is light brown, flip it carefully and cook it on the other side for another minute. And that's it! Crepes are best

served hot with fruit and whipped cream, but what you decide to put on your crepes is up to you!'

Paragraph two

'I have seen quite a few tree houses in my time, but this was the comfiest treehouse I ever had the pleasure to visit. Opening the small, bright blue door, I shucked my shoes off before entering the little space nestled in the oak's firm spreading branches. The red and black rug spread over the wood planks felt warm and soft beneath my feet. To my right, a bright blue beanbag beckoned, plumped, and ready to sink back into. As I took a seat, I looked around. By my elbow, a small electric lantern on a tiny side table lit up the space with a golden glow. Beyond it, an antique bookcase with only two shelves held a variety of books and toys neatly arranged in a row. Beside the bookcase, an equally compact chest lay propped open, revealing blankets, pillows, and other stuffed animals. Opposite my corner, two more beanbags sat empty. The rest of the room was filled with a variety of sports equipment hastily jumbled in a long open wood box. Honestly, it was the kind of treehouse I could only dream of when I was a child.'

Paragraph three

'Sheridan Le Fanu's titular character Carmilla explores Gothic anxieties about the shadow self. If Laura represents the best of us, Carmilla is the hidden shadow, the heimlich of our psychology. A mirror image to the blonde-haired and blue-eyed Laura, Carmilla's dark hair and dark eyes provides a physical representation of the mental and experiential contrast apparent in both. Unlike the pure and demure Laura, Carmilla's age has gifted her maturity, worldliness, and experience. She is able to move in a variety of social circles and take on many identities (73, 77). Spielsdorf describes Carmilla with admiration, saying that her conversation was interesting without being vapid or gossipy (79). Unfortunately, the abilities and intelligence of Carmilla are complicated by her need for blood, her predatory behavior toward Laura, and her manipulative techniques to gain a foothold in society. Ultimately, Carmilla must be vanquished, but the impact of her presence remains. Through Carmilla, Sheridan Le Fanu uses the Gothic to recognize the necessary energy inherent in our darker natures, but at the same presents a warning: the darkest parts of us may be vanquished, but it is never truly gone.'

Paragraph four

'It was going to be a fun day at the beach. Terry just knew it. Catching sight of blue water between the trees, Terry's walk broke into an all-out run as he raced down the small forest path to the edge of the lake. Sunlight glancing a golden path on the water beckoned irresistibly. The young boy paused only for a moment. Before his mother could get a word out, Terry pulled off his shirt, socks, and shoes, dumping them into a pile on the sand. With a shriek of delight, he threw himself into the water and yelled with shock as a cold wave hit him in the face. Standing up and spluttering, Terry turned around, wiping the water out of his eyes, only to realize that his older brother and dad were watching him with barely contained laughter. He grinned and shouted, jumping up and down. This day was going to be the best!'

Snapshot

There are four major types of paragraphs—descriptive, narrative, expository, and persuasive. All four can be used for various situations, from academic to professional to personal projects. However, all rely on organization and solid knowledge or research in order to provide clear communication of the topic. Using a simple formula, you can organize your paragraph into three specific parts: topic sentence, detail sentences, and a conclusion or transition sentence. Keeping your carefully created outline and your audience in mind, you'll know what paragraph you should be using as well as when you should start a new one. Now you are ready to try writing a paragraph for yourself!

Chapter 7
Step 3: Composing Your Powerful Paragraph Using Study Skills

You are walking down an empty road. The gray pavement beneath your feet stretches off toward an empty horizon. On either side, wilderness stretches beneath a bright blue sky. As you turn to look back, you can see how far you've come far off in the distance. You've left your starting point behind. It's the perfect moment to pause, to recognize the path you have taken to get here. Taking stock of everything you have learned, you know that you're more than ready to take the next step. You're ready to push forward.

What has changed? You understand your strengths and weaknesses. You know which study skills and habits you already have and which ones you need to develop further. You have created a supportive study environment that will provide you with the energy, focus, and comfort you require. With your practical, step-by-step study plan laid out, your life, and schedule, have been optimized to encourage your study and writing needs. Once your preparations were complete, you revisited the role, function, styles, and set up of paragraphs. Now, it's time to write the first draft of your own powerful paragraph!

Getting Started

Many people might just start writing a paragraph, but if you want to increase your efficiency or focus, it's a good idea to think about your writing goals, audience, and your topic. Once you decide on your writing goals and audience, it's time to choose the specific topic you want to write about.

During this phase, it's easy to overlook something very crucial. Many writers end up writing about something they don't like or care about. This is a big problem when you are writing for school. However, if possible, try to choose an approach or perspective you feel strongly about or are already familiar with. If you are invested in what you're writing about, you're more likely to finish your project.

So, sit down, think up a topic you want to write about, and brainstorm content for it. What are you going to write about? It's not so easy to just start writing about a process, event, or scene. Instead, begin to outline your ideas as you consider these questions:

- What could you say about this topic?
- Is this a descriptive, narrative, expository, or persuasive paragraph?
- Which details should you share and which should you leave out?
- What argument could you make about this topic? What opinion do you have on this topic?
- How are you going to organize the data or details?

With these questions answered, you will be able to start sketching an outline. At this stage, you can begin to recheck your resources. Searching online and visiting your library is a great way to understand what sources and authorities you can rely on for support, especially when it comes to academic projects.

Try it Out Now!

Choose a topic you are interested in and answer the questions above. If you're working on an academic or professional project, choose source materials that you might rely on, as support, for your data. This may involve making up an early Reference list.

Creating an Outline

Now that you understand what direction you want to head in, you are ready to outline your ideas by organizing the data and details you have gathered. Your outline, forming the backbone of your paragraph, will give you a track to follow as you write, helping you move through the writing phase even quicker than usual. Let's take a look at two different stages of outlining that you can do.

Roughly Sketched Outlines

As you figure out what you want to write, you can start sketching out some ideas. This rough outline can help you understand where your research is weighted. Do you know more about one idea or argument than another? What is your weakest point? Which part of the paragraph has less information? These kinds of questions are fundamental if you are working on a persuasive paragraph or project.

By thinking through these questions, you should be able to create a shortlist outlining the points you might want to use. Feel free to add question marks or notes to yourself in the process because you are just roughly sketching your ideas out at this stage. If we think about the Mars paragraph we looked at in the previous chapter; the roughly sketched outline might look something like this:

- Mars is a place where we could live
- atmosphere
- temperature
- weather systems
- distance from Earth
- rotation on-axis
- four seasons?
- a year on Mars?
- gravity

You can see that this outline has no real details but provides a general direction the writer might want to go in. Mind maps, lists, and other brainstorming techniques can help you think of ideas you may want to tackle in your paragraph. Once the list is complete, it's time to get researching!

Detailed Outlines With the P.E.E/P.E.A Method

What if you are writing a persuasive or expository essay for a school assignment? How about scientific or literary reports? For these writing projects, it's a good idea to review your detailed outline and make sure that you're providing explanation and analysis where required. Where do you do that? It's pretty easy when you follow the P.E.E (or P.E.A) method. Let's find out how to focus your outline on the most important part of an essay's paragraph—making your point and evidence matter.

(P) Point

Looking at our sample paragraph on Mars, there are a lot of points being made. If you use the P.E.E/P.E.A method, you want to ensure that your paragraph's sub-points are straightforward statements of facts that you can support with evidence. In this sample, the writer has changed the detailed outline points into more complete sentences:

- Mars, a close neighbor to Earth, offers a challenge to living on another planet.
- The atmosphere and weather systems are less diverse.
- Days are similar to Earth, but years on Mars last way longer.
- Temperatures are less comfortable for us.
- Gravity isn't the same either.

Now that we have some general statements, it's time to add the evidence you have discovered during your time researching.

(E) Evidence

Whether it's specific facts, anecdotes, or examples, it is a must-have for most academic papers. To a large degree, the data you use requires proper documentation and citations in the text, either through summarization or direct quotes. You can add the citations to the outline as well. The sample below, an appropriate outline for a conversational, yet informative blog post, will usually not refer to sources in the reading. That is because interjecting page numbers and authors often breaks the flow for readers.

- Mars, a close neighbor to Earth, offers a challenge to living on another planet.
- The atmosphere and weather systems are less diverse.
- no dense atmosphere
- fewer weather systems
- slow-moving tornados
- Days are similar to Earth, but years on Mars last way longer.
- days: 24.5 hours long
- years: 687 days long
- Temperatures are less comfortable for us.
- warmest temperature: 70 degrees F
- coldest temperature: -225 degrees F
- Gravity isn't the same either.
- less mass = less gravity = less weight on Mars

With the details of your research added, you just need to add one more set of details before you start writing: explanation or analysis.

(E/A) Explanation or Analysis

So what if Mars has fewer weather systems or longer year cycles? What does that even mean? Explaining or analyzing your data is an excellent way to show your reader that you haven't just understood the material but are ready to apply or explain the information to others. When you can provide an answer to the "so what," you are able to show your ability to analyze and draw conclusions. If you can bring a fresh perspective to the essay question or report assignment, the more interesting it will be for your audience. But the most important thing to focus on is showing your critical thinking skills. This might mean that you provided an evidence-based set of opinions or argumentations. It might involve drawing connections between two ideas in order to arrive at another set of ideas, presenting a new path for other academics to explore.

In our Mars example, after the evidence and details have been made, we can draw a conclusion about the data we've shared. For example, we might say that Mars is not currently habitable, a point that will lead nicely into the next paragraph.

- Explanation/Analysis: There are a lot of difficulties to be overcome before we can safely settle on Mars.

For this paragraph, we could provide explanations for each sub-point or add an explanation or analysis at the end of the paragraph. Most explanations and analyses are located at the end of the paragraph before the transition or conclusion sentence. Now, your outline is truly done!

Your Turn!

Look through all of the notes you have made as well as your Reference list. How are you going to organize your ideas and data? Which details do you want to tackle first? You can try out different ways to organize your research with a roughly sketched outline before settling on your final one. Take the time to make an even more detailed outline using the P.E.E/P.E.A method if your paragraph involves juggling sources and a lot of data.

Getting a Clearer Picture

It's time to sit down and write your paragraph. With all of the preparation finished, you can try writing the first draft for your powerful paragraph. But before that, it might be a good idea to review what makes a great paragraph, practice recognizing the good from the bad, then—go for the goal of writing your best attempt at a first draft.

After studying what a paragraph is and how it functions, you probably have a pretty clear idea about what a good paragraph looks like. It should have a comprehensive topic sentence, on-topic evidence statements, sentences focused on explanation or analysis, and a clear conclusion or transition sentence. As we go through the following four writing samples, two well-written and two poorly written paragraphs, try to note the four expected parts of a good paragraph as well as the organization and focus. You can ask yourself these questions as you go, before reading the paragraph notes.

- What is the topic sentence? Is it at the beginning?
- Is there enough evidence or support? Where are they placed?
- Has P.E.E/P.E.A been used to think or consider the topic in detail?
- What is the conclusion or transition sentence? Is it at the end?

Example of a Good Paragraph: In Praise of Cats

'Furthermore, compared to other animals, cats require much less maintenance. Your house cat will not need very expensive equipment like tanks, filters, or food. Aside from your pet's vaccination shots, your cat's shopping list will only include a few cat toys, a scratching post, cat food, and a litter box. Unlike dogs, you don't have to walk your cat, but you can encourage more physical activity by providing a cat jungle gym. As long as your house is large enough, your house cat will get the exercise they need. Additionally, well-trained cats will use their litter box, which means that you don't have to worry about taking your pet out. Although it's recommended that you change your cat litter at least twice a week, this is a far cry from the daily, sometimes twice daily, bathroom walks required from dog owners. Overall, if you are seeking the perfect animal companion, cats are the furry friends you can care for easily with minimal impact on your wallet. The only question that remains is: which cat is going to suit you best?'

. . .

LOOKING CLOSELY AT THIS PARAGRAPH, we can see that it has a clear topic sentence that determines the focus of the paragraph to be about cat maintenance. As a compare and contrast paragraph, the body of evidence focuses on three main points—equipment, exercise, and pet care. The takeaway analysis results in the writer advocating for cats as an excellent option for house pets due to their easy care and low cost. It ends with a question posed to the reader, which will lead into the next section on cat breeds and types. At various points, you can see how transition phrases and words throughout the paragraph encourage logical flow, such as furthermore, additionally, and overall.

Example of a Good Paragraph: The Life of Nikola Tesla

'Leading up to his best years of work, Nikola Tesla had to work very hard and sacrifice much. Born in 1856 in Croatia, his early life on the family farm was far from easy. The death of his brother Daniel shocked young Tesla, who began to experience visions. After completing school and moving to Paris for work, in 1884, Tesla migrated to the United States alone, where he worked for Thomas Edison. That might sound like a

dream job, and although he improved Edison's DC dynamos, he did not receive the wages he had been promised. Unfortunately, starting his own company was difficult, and Tesla ended up digging ditches for two dollars a day for a short period of time. Between the difficulties of mental trauma, immigration, and professional exploitation, Tesla had much to overcome as a scientist and inventor. Still, his dedication to knowledge eventually brought him to the public eye. From then on, Tesla's work as an inventor always involved a struggle between balancing finances and interests, but he was only just getting started.'

IN THIS WELL-WRITTEN PARAGRAPH, we have a general introduction to the main idea being discussed in terms of Nikola Tesla's life. The paragraph then follows a logical, linear path from Tesla's birth to his later years of work. It is followed up with a point being made about his life, which supports the main idea of the topic sentence. Finally, to serve as a transition, the last sentence suggests that the next paragraph will be about Tesla's later work. Throughout the paragraph, you can see that a mixture of simple, complex, and compound sentence structures are present, encouraging flow and interest as well as giving the paragraph some formality.

Example of a Bad Paragraph: My Favorite Time of Year

'Fall is the best time to enjoy a soothing pumpkin latte with a large dollop of whipped cream. Valentine's Day is such a romantic holiday. Halloween and Thanksgiving are cozy holidays that I absolutely look forward to. Then there's the weather, particularly in September and early October, where it is warm but not super hot. On those days, I like to go for walks, even when it's drizzling out. It's great to just enjoy the scuffle of your boots among the fallen, colored leaves. Which reminds me—the changing colors of the leaves is always a sight to behold in the fall. Really, fall is my favorite time of year.'

I THINK it's easy to see that this paragraph is a hot mess! Where did it go wrong? For starters, the topic sentence is at the end of the paragraph instead of being set at the beginning. Without a clear topic sentence, the paragraph appears to meander from idea to idea. On top of that, you can see that the explanation and analysis sentences of the paragraph are completely absent. Without a proper conclusion sentence at the end, the paragraph feels like it is slowly petering off without any purpose. Even if this was written for a blog, many readers might feel like the paragraph is choppy and disjointed since there are no transition phrases or words. Finally, spelling, punctuation, and grammatical errors still need to be fixed. How would you improve this paragraph?

Example of a Bad Paragraph: The True Heartbeat of Jaws

'K.I.S.S. Keep it simple, stupid. That's the idea John Williams had when he composed the score for Jaws in 1975. The famous composer's score for the tense drama film uses a two-note motif to increase the tension in the shark scenes. The notes are usually E and F or F and F#. They are simple alternating notes, they feel like they will never stop. The effect is that the shark is an unstoppable machine. When the shark finally shows itself, the full theme of the film springs to life and culminates in a fearful revelation. It's no wonder that Williams won an Oscar for his work on Jaws.'

. . .

THIS MIGHT SEEM like an interesting paragraph to read, but a lot is going on here that isn't the greatest. For starters, where is the topic sentence? Without a topic sentence, there is no focus for any analysis or explanation. Instead, the reader is just given information in a disjointed kind of way. The lack of flow is made worse by all of the simple sentences, which also rely heavily on simple, passive verbs like 'is' and 'are.' Then, there is the audience to consider. If this is written for a blog, the conversational style would work, but the tone and style of writing for an academic paper at university is too informal. Keeping this in mind, in what way would you tweak this paragraph?

Fixing these last two paragraphs might be pretty easy, but now the real test of your studies is coming up! Having reviewed some samples of well-written and poorly written paragraphs, you probably have a good idea of how to move forward with your own paragraph. It's time to apply all of the knowledge you have gained and the preparation you set up beforehand. Check out the section below for some writing prompts and a further paragraph analysis challenge.

In Summary

Top Tip: Outline Your Paragraph Beforehand!

Using the P.E.E/P.E.A method, create a detailed outline that you can follow easily as you write your paragraphs. Outlining your entire project beforehand will help you maintain focus and feel more prepared to finish the project efficiently. Not only will you gain motivation, but you'll also be able to analyze the extent of your research, and troubleshoot weak areas in this and your argumentation, early on.

CHALLENGE!

Before you sit down and write your own paragraph, take time to review the following two paragraphs by yourself. As examples of good paragraphs, what are they doing right? How is the information organized? How are the topic sentences, evidence statements, and analysis used? Are there proper transition words to help keep the flow of ideas smooth? Given the audiences mentioned, are the tone, word choice, and writing style appropriate?

. . .

CASUAL AUDIENCE:

'If Samsung's Note series smartphone screens didn't give you the size you wanted, the most innovative takes on foldable phones are finally hitting the market. First on the list- is Samsung. We already have the Fold series, which boasts a massive screen. On the other hand, Xiaomi has also been one of Samsung's fiercest competitors, putting out its Mi Mix Fold phone, which is almost the size of a small tablet. Furthermore, companies like Oppo and Google are also pursuing large screen options, hoping to bring their own touch to the next great leap in telecommunication. Although quite a few smartphone development teams will require time to iterate on and devise alternative prototypes to the folding phone, in the next few years, increased competition and cheaper means to achieve larger screens will lead to affordable options. Before you know it, you will be able to open your phone and stream online content without lowering the quality and detail.'

ACADEMIC AUDIENCE:

'Firstly, Watson's initial description of Sherlock Holmes links the detective to the concept of man as an

intelligent, unmatched machine. Since emotions get in the way of perspective and observation, Sherlock eschews emotions. The doctor states that Sherlock is "the most perfect reasoning and observing machine that the world has seen" (Doyle, 3). To a certain extent, this divorce from internal emotions also gives Sherlock the ability to move through the metropolis like a chameleon. In "A Scandal in Bohemia," Sherlock can maintain very believable disguises to further his investigations. Moreover, his ability to remain rational gives him the power to think quickly and predict human behavior, as we can see from his guesses about Watson's home life (3-4), the client's identity (5), and some of Adler's actions (11). To Sir Arthur Conan Doyle's audience, Sherlock Holmes appears to be the epitome of modern man, completely logical and agential. However, beneath the veneer of competence and dominance, Sherlock's clash with Irene Adler calls into question the ideal of the modern machine.'

Now it's time to sit down and write your own paragraph. Hooray! Make sure that you have set aside at least half an hour of quiet in your best study environment. After reviewing your notes and outlines, you can finally get to crafting your paragraph's first draft.

Snapshot

Writing a powerful paragraph requires quite a bit of preparation. After considering the topic you have chosen, brainstorming ideas, and doing preliminary research, writing the rough outline of a draft will help you focus on where to do further research and how to organize your thoughts. The P.E.E/P.E.A method organizes your paragraph into points-evidence-explanation/analysis, which will show your ability to think critically and bring new perspectives to your readers. When reviewing well-written and poorly written paragraphs, once again, you're reminded of what important factors make a paragraph great. It's now time to get writing yourself!

Chapter 8
Step 4: Fleshing out Your Paragraph Without Fluff or Waffling

There's nothing better than hanging out on a lakeside restaurant patio under a warm summer sun. Well, if you gave me a dessert waffle and an iced latte, it'd make the day even better because, after all, it's the little things in life that add to our lived experiences. The opposite is true of writing, though.

Waffles are great for breakfast or dessert, NOT a good paragraph, so avoid adding fluff at all costs. Try not to add unnecessary sentences or details as much as possible. That is why one of the most challenging things in writing is keeping on track and improving flow while maintaining clarity. We might think that more is better, and that's true—if you are talking about a summertime patio hangout. But when it comes to writing, less is more. An important question to ask during the substantive editing phase is, "What is the clearest, most concise way to share my ideas?"

Keeping on Track

Now that you've finished your first draft of a paragraph, it's time to look through the content and tweak any substantive changes before proofreading and spell-checking. Substantive editing requires changing and tweaking the content and major sections of your writing. During this phase, you should look through your paragraphs, sources, and sentences, noting any inconsistencies or disorganization in the points. Consider these questions as you double-check your work:

- Am I following the outline I had written? Why or why not?
- Does my paragraph have all of the parts of a typical paragraph? Have I followed the standard paragraph structure?
- Am I using P.E.E/P.E.A correctly?
- Does the logical organization of the paragraph feel right or make sense?

How to Write a Paragraph Using Study Skills

- Do I have enough factual support for my argument or opinion?
- Do any points lack sufficient evidence?
- Are my citations correct?
- Do I have enough sources? Are there any sentences missing citations?

With the basic body of the paragraph edited, you can consider other ways of organizing your writing project, especially if it's going to be part of a larger whole. For example, when it comes to organization, you might want to use sub-headings to make the logical flow of your writing more crystal clear for your readers. Blogs and certain essay formats, like APA, encourage sub-headings as a way to let the reader know which sections tackle which part of the topic.

Another important factor to keep an eye out for is the issue of fluff or waffling. Once again, waffles are great for dessert, less so for writing! Ask yourself if any sentences repeat information unnecessarily. Have you said something three different times in three different ways? Time to get cutting! Every sentence written should supplement further information, explanations, or analysis. This way, the reader doesn't feel like they're wasting their time reading the same details over and over. Instead, you're offering them a clear-cut, direct form of communication meant to enhance their knowledge base and life.

Improving Flow

It's not enough to simply get to the point, though. For many writers, academic and professional, the art of writing is more than just sharing information. You want to encourage your reader to stay with you, read to the end of your blog or essay, and come away with something meaningful. Great writing techniques that improve flow can help hook and then keep your audience reading. Transition words and sentence structures are two significant areas that can impact flow. So, how do you use them correctly?

Transition Words

Transition words, or words that help you move from one idea to another, can signal to a reader that something is coming. It might be a contrasting idea, a supplemental idea, or even a summation of the whole point. Properly used, transition words can smooth out the logical flow of your outline from one sentence to another. Check out the following lists for a variety of transition words!

Do you want to contrast two ideas? Let's say you want to say that Mars has little to no atmosphere, but with the help of specified domes for living areas, could have artificial sources of oxygen. You will want to use one of the following transition words.

- although
- conversely
- different from
- even though
- however
- in comparison
- in contrast
- nevertheless
- on the contrary
- on the other hand
- still
- whereas
- yet

How about adding to or building on an idea? In terms of Mars's atmosphere problem, you want to suggest that encouraging plant life on Mars could help form organic sources of oxygen. In that case, you will want to use one of the following transition words:

- additionally
- again
- also
- another reason
- as well as
- for example
- furthermore
- in addition
- in fact
- likewise
- moreover
- similarly
- whereas

What if you want to introduce the cause or effect of something? For our Mars example, what if we wanted to say that a combination of artificial dome technology, and organic plant farming, might lead to improved oxygen levels for colonizers on Mars? One of the following transition words could help lead to that point.

- accordingly

How to Write a Paragraph Using Study Skills

- as a result
- because
- consequently
- due to
- for the most part
- for this purpose
- for this reason
- in this situation
- otherwise
- particularly
- undoubtedly or no doubt
- usually

Do you want to explain a process or tell a story? Perhaps you want to outline the steps that a Martian colony would have to take to enhance the poor atmosphere on the planet. You can use the following transition words to order the events by sequence.

- at first
- eventually
- first
- first of all
- in the first place
- initially
- next

- previously
- second
- subsequently
- then
- third
- to begin with

What about wrapping up an idea or starting a conclusion paragraph? Does your paragraph on Mars end with a final reminder about the long process required to provide workable solutions for life support on the red planet? In that case, you would want to use one of these transition words.

- as a final point
- as I have argued
- as previously stated
- at last
- finally
- given these points
- in conclusion
- in short
- in sum
- in summary
- it is clear that
- last but not least

- lastly
- overall
- to conclude
- to resume
- to return to my main argument
- to summarize

That being said, after learning about transition words, you might be excited to start using them everywhere. I would recommend incorporating them carefully. Don't try to use them for every single sentence. Usually, it's best to have three or so transition words to help a single paragraph along. Any more would sound strange and overused, making your sentences boring and too similar.

Sentence Structure

Sentences, which are the essential bones of your paragraph, can also make or break your reading flow. Using transition words can help your sentences move smoothly from one idea to the next. Although, it's a great idea to change the structure from time to time to make it sound different. Aim to change the pacing with a mixture of long and short sentences.

Writing a punchy short sentence might be easy, but combining ideas to form a longer sentence while maintaining clarity is more difficult. I recommend you check the glossary for "sentence structure" and brush up on the differences between simple, compound, complex, and compound-complex sentences. With these four sentence structures in your toolkit, you can control the flow of your paragraph so much easier!

So you know how to change up a sentence, but let's not forget understanding what words to choose is just as important!

Pursuing Clarity

Not all words are the same, and a writer needs to know which words to use and when. Since writing for an audience is focused on communicating something, clarity is a major goal. That requires an understanding of synonyms and antonyms, the impact of connotation, and the power of strong verbs. Sometimes you might be wondering what word to use, or maybe you realize you keep repeating words and would like to find alternative options. You reach for a thesaurus, and... What do you do now? Do you just randomly pick something? That doesn't seem right, does it?

You might know all about synonyms and antonyms. After all, that's what mainly fills a thesaurus. However, connotations need to be kept in mind as well as the known denotations of a word. While the word 'denotation' means the literal meaning of a word, connotations essentially refer to the second meaning, feelings, or ideas that the word suggests. Connotations of any language can sometimes change over time, so they can be rather slippery to get a hold of, especially for non-native speakers and writers. For example, suppose you were to describe a person as being overweight. In that case, the adjective 'overweight' is relatively neutral, but if you called them 'full-figured' or 'fat,' the emotions linked to the description would be different. As a result, changing up word choices with synonyms does require some thought and an understanding of their connotations. Using a dictionary, in this case, is a great secondary resource to figure out whether the word you want to use holds the connotations you require.

For verb use, you might also find yourself using the same ones repeatedly. Are your sentences relying on 'is' and 'are' all the time? Does your sentence structure overuse passive verb use? Stative verbs, like 'is' and 'are,' can feel very familiar and reliable, but using action verbs will provide energy within your writing. Your readers won't be bored and instead will find themselves caught up in your ideas! Consider some of these active verbs that you can use, depending on the logical pattern you wish to attempt.

- allude to
- assume
- allows
- confirms
- concludes
- determines
- demonstrates
- discovers
- establishes
- explains
- explores
- encourages
- illustrates
- indicates
- initiates
- improves
- leads to
- pinpoints

How to Write a Paragraph Using Study Skills

- presents
- prompts
- provides
- provokes
- questions
- represents
- results
- reveals
- signifies
- stimulates
- supplies
- underscores
- validates

After reviewing the verbs you used and switching some for active verbs, you can also check that you aren't relying too heavily on passive verbs. Passive verbs shift the focus from the subject of the sentence to its objects, whether they are direct objects or objects of prepositions, etc. On the other hand, active verbs keep the energy focused on the subject and increase momentum for readers. Consider these two sentences.

Sentence 1: *The man threw the ball.*

Sentence 2: *The ball was thrown by the man.*

Which sentence has more energy? Which one feels like it's full of action? Sentence one, right? That's because its verb, 'threw,' is an active verb, allowing the subject (the man) to do something. Compare that to Sentence two. Sure, there are more words in it, but it's better to avoid unnecessarily padding your work. You also don't want the energy of an active verb diluted by shifting the focus to the direct object.

Keep these tips in mind to hone your word choices. You'll discover that shaping your paragraph will not only get a lot easier but also result in clearer and smoother writing. You have removed fluff, improved your sentence flow, and increased clarity on the topic with stronger word choices. Now that substantive editing is complete, you can celebrate the creation of your paragraph's second draft!

In Summary

Top Tip: Use Transition Words!

Choosing the right transition words for your paragraph isn't always easy. You will need to consider whether you're trying to contrast, add to, continue, or summarize an idea. However, with the proper placement and use of transition words, the flow and clarity of your organized points will make the process of reading easier and more enjoyable for your readers.

Challenge!

Now that you have finished your first draft, it's time to check the content of your writing with some substantive editing. Use this checklist to verify you've covered all of your bases before continuing to the next stage of editing and proofreading.

- Have I followed my outline?
- Did I use the P.E.E/P.E.A method for explaining and analyzing the information I'm sharing?
- Have I inserted unnecessary or unproven opinions?
- Are there any sentences that are unnecessary or filled with fluff?
- Is the flow of the paragraph smooth?
- Have I used transition words correctly?
- What words could I replace with stronger, more vivid adjectives or verbs?

- Are too many of my sentences passive or simple?

Snapshot

Now that you have finished your first draft, it's time to check the bones of your research and writing, making sure that every sentence covers the outline you created. Furthermore, you will need to question whether unnecessary fluff sentences exist that need removing. After you improve the flow of your paragraph, with varied and well-placed transition words and sentences, double-check your word choices with the careful use of a thesaurus and dictionary! Finally, read through your paragraph to assess whether you're relying too heavily on stative or passive verbs. Change any as required to give your paragraph more energy and interest!

Chapter 9
Step 5: Using Study Skills To Proofread and Edit Your Paragraph to Perfection

You've laid the foundation and built the walls of your house. You might feel like it's time to celebrate. Go ahead and rest up, but remember, your work is far from done! Think about it. Would you want to live in a house made with just bricks and concrete? What about the paint, flooring, doors, and all the small details that transform the space into a cozy home? In the end, the small things that decorate your home give it personality and comfort, which is sure to provide hospitality to visitors. Similarly, polishing your writing will allow you to provide an enjoyable reading experience for your audience.

After making substantive edits on your first draft, it's time to give your second draft some polish. Copy-editing involves small-scale changes to your writing, like checking your spelling or grammar. Although you may have already performed these changes as you worked through your first two drafts, a final polish is always a good idea. Where do you start? Before trying out any of the tips and tricks mentioned below, set your draft aside for a few days. This is why it is imperative to use your time management skills to plan and prepare enough time before your deadline to proofread and edit your work. With a fresh eye, you can take your time to catch the smaller errors in your writing.

Zoom in With Copy-Editing

It's time to focus on your spelling, punctuation, and grammar. Your first instinct may be to use a spell-checker, but make sure you don't "auto-correct all." Instead, double-check every error brought to your attention and consider the context. You don't want special jargon or specific academic words (not familiar to the writing software database) to be replaced by inappropriate, even if correctly spelled, words.

How to Write a Paragraph Using Study Skills

For starters, you can begin by checking your grammar. Problem areas of grammar usually lie within how you use nouns, adverbs, and verbs. You need to take into consideration whether your nouns and verbs agree. For example, plural nouns may change how a verb is spelled or used in a sentence. In other instances, you will want to double-check whether you have accidentally switched from the second to a third-person perspective. If you've been using 'we' and 'us' at the beginning of the paragraph, it would be rather jarring to switch to another perspective. Adverb placement can also get tricky because many adverbs can be moved around for different effects. As a result, it's important to take your time to check each of your sentences to remove as many grammatical errors or inconsistencies as possible.

Next, you should go through your document slowly, looking for spelling errors. Spelling will require you to check your document carefully, keeping an eye out for misspelled words and academic jargon. You will also need to watch for words that are not misspelled but aren't the words you intended to use. In these cases, the words won't necessarily show as an error, resulting in a sentence that doesn't make sense. Mistakes like this can be easy to miss, but using the proofreading techniques below will help you catch even these difficult-to-find errors.

Finally, it's time to check your punctuation! Punctuation, which involves the use of periods, commas, and other marks, helps improve clarity and brings order to sentence structure. The longer the sentence, the more punctuation comes into play, so it's often a significant factor in academic assignments. Like spelling, it might be tempting to go the easy route, but take the time to double-check your punctuation. You'll be able to triple-check your writing's content and flow at the same time!

Proofreading Techniques

Now that you're ready to proofread and edit, you might be wondering, "How do I check my work if auto-correct isn't recommended?". The good news is that quite a few techniques can help you bring a fresh perspective to your written work. Unfortunately, these methods require time and effort, so you should schedule copy-editing in advance. You can try some or all of these approaches, using each run to target a specific focus, whether it's grammar, spelling, or punctuation.

Reading Aloud

In a quiet study zone where you can hear yourself easily, take time to read your paragraph aloud slowly. As you move through the sentences, correct any mistakes as required. While reading aloud, you might realize that the pacing may be off, and a sentence here and there might need to be tweaked.

Pros: It slows you down, so you notice small errors you may have missed.

Cons: You need a quiet area where you can hear yourself and not disrupt other students.

Reading Backwards

Sometimes all you need is a fresh perspective. What better way to look at your writing than from the end to the beginning? Turn to the last page and work your way backward, sentence by sentence. It might feel strange at first, but this technique is sure to help you catch misspellings and punctuation errors. However, since you're reading in reverse, organization issues and research weaknesses won't be apparent.

Pros: It will increase spelling and punctuation awareness.

Cons: It won't help you pick up other issues with your writing.

Rereading Later

With a deadline looming, your gut instinct might be to rush, but in reality, the last thing you should do is pack all of your copy-editing into a couple of hours. If you give yourself the required amount of time, preferably two to three days, you'll have some much-needed space from your writing. After doing the first run of substantive editing, you should put it down to reread after a few hours. The longer you space out your edits, the more chance you have to return with a more objective perspective on what you have written.

Pros: It will give you a fresh look at your writing.

Cons: Requires time (at least 5 hours).

Peer Review

Are you tired of looking at the same words over and over again? Who wouldn't be, right? One way to get an objective look at your paragraph or writing project is to ask a friend, family member, or fellow student. Often pacing and organization that feels right or makes sense to you will confuse your readers, so getting a second opinion will usually help. Of course, this means that your editor needs to know what makes for a good essay or blog. This means that if you choose your editor poorly, you might end up with bad advice or not the advice you need.

Pros: A new pair of eyes may catch things you have missed or areas that are confusing.

Cons: You might end up with a poor editing job that will make things worse.

Don't Forget Your Toolkit!

Whether you're substantive or copy-editing your paragraph, the entire process requires you to develop and mature your study skills. While following these powerful paragraph steps, you've already started to explore a variety of study skills, which will provide you with tools to polish your writing from here on out. Even during the editing phase, study skills are incredibly crucial.

As mentioned before, clear communication is a crucial study skill achieved by understanding how to communicate with others. You might link communication skills to understanding how to work with fellow students or teachers. However, it also requires a strong knowledge of grammar and the use of varied sentence structures to connect your readers to your ideas in an easy-to-follow way. Knowing and targeting your audience plays a crucial role in clear communication. It will affect your writing style and tone, as well as what information you include in your project.

While reading through the data you've chosen to discuss in your essay, report, or blog, you'll need to rely on study skills linked to detail-oriented work. During the substantive editing phase, you'll have to make sure that all points of your outline are covered and that your research is complete. Double-checking your bibliography and the way you cite your sources can be time-consuming, but eventually, you will discover your own way to keep track of the data you're using. Whether you rely on websites to create reference lists or a plethora of sticky notes, study skills will help you learn how to keep organized and stay on track.

Technology is always an excellent tool for organization, fact-checking, and correction. Then again, it can often be a source of misinformation or fail to catch your errors. Relying thoughtlessly on technology causes you to waste time going backward to cover ground you might have fixed earlier—if you had just slowed down. When crunch time comes, you might be tempted to just autocorrect or grab the top-most link on the Google search you started. Study skills, however, will give you the ability to assess what technological software and techniques will help and which ones are less likely to support your needs.

Few writers are truly able to edit and correct themselves alone. Most require some sort of support, whether it is from a friend, family member, or fellow student. Teachers and parents can often give reliable, constructive feedback as well, but it's up to you to learn from your mistakes. Study skills such as recognizing and using constructive criticism, and breaking down goals into achievable steps, are crucial strengths you'll need in order to break through the difficulty of the editing phase. Time after time, we start out feeling confident after writing an essay or blog post, only to realize halfway through editing that things are worse than they had seemed. Don't give up! Instead, give yourself a breather, let someone else look it over, and return to your writing with a fresh eye and a willingness to make changes as necessary. When you can divorce yourself from your work, you'll be able to note what needs tweaking before coming up with solutions for the errors that have cropped up.

Ultimately, all of this takes time. That is why time management and organization remain the top two study skills everyone should develop. These two skills alone will help you understand how to manage expectations, set yourself up for success, and form positive study and writing habits. Perfect for balancing work, life, and writing! Recognizing your goals and breaking them down into manageable steps requires you to be honest about your available time and energy. When you recognize your limits, you'll be able to understand how much time you can set aside for writing. With a chance to form positive writing and study habits, you'll discover the path to long-term success!

In Summary

Top Tip: Get a Second Opinion!

If you have someone you trust to copy or substantive

edit, make sure to include time for a peer review in your writing and study schedule. A different, outside perspective is sure to pick up errors or breaks in logic that you have overlooked. Who should you pick? Make sure that the editor you choose will be able to set time aside to go through your writing thoughtfully and carefully. You also want to choose someone who understands grammar and punctuation as well. With a reliable partner, you'll be able to get a second opinion before sharing your work.

Challenge!

Review the paragraph you wrote. Whether you're writing by hand or on a computer, go through sentence by sentence using one of the four techniques above. If you're working on a computer, when you notice an error line in your writing software, try to figure out what might need changing before using the correcting function. As you edit, follow the techniques in this order:

- Read through once and make changes.
- Pause and set aside.
- Read through again aloud.

- Set your writing aside for a few more hours.
- Read it a third time, backward.
- Give it to a friend or fellow student to check.
- Read through one last time and consider it done!

You are now ready to share your paragraph!

Snapshot

Copy-editing involves a more detailed, smaller-scale process focused primarily on grammar, spelling, and punctuation. Using a variety of proofreading techniques, like reading aloud, reading backward, or relying on peer review, writers can eventually polish their work and prepare it for a wider audience. In the process of editing, many kinds of study skills are used, ranging from data organization to proper use of technology and time management. Like other steps in the writing process, if you have scheduled yourself enough time to properly devote to editing, you'll discover that the outcome is sure to be stellar!

If you're enjoying this book so far, kindly leave a review sharing your thoughts using the QR code below!

Chapter 10
Applying Your Newfound Skills to Longer Writing Tasks

As a toddler, we all figured out how to place one foot in front of the other. Sure, in the beginning, we relied on our parents' hand or the edge of a coffee table but eventually, we knew how to stagger across the floor on our own. One step at a time, we broadened our horizons, and with practice, learned how to run. Now that we're older, the same fundamentals of walking remain with us, no matter where we go.

Understanding how to formulate a good sentence and paragraph is no different. These simple processes provide you with the necessary framework for bigger and better things. With these basics under your belt, positive study habits, and well-developed study skills, you'll be able to take on larger and more complex writing projects, including essays and even novels! It all begins with a well-researched outline and well-crafted paragraphs. All you need to know now is how to use your study skills to prepare and organize for the ultimate writing challenge: an essay.

Approaching an Essay

There's no need to learn anything new. That's the good news! You have all the tools and skills that you need to figure out, prepare for, and execute an A+ essay. Of course, it all begins with good old organization and time management, the key fundamentals of all study skills. Less complex essays require at least two to four weeks to complete, including research, but longer academic papers can take up to an entire school year, if not longer! Fortunately, the same approaches we applied to writing paragraphs can also be used for tackling longer writing projects. But first, we need to start with the obvious challenge: the essay question.

The First Hurdle: The Big Q

When facing a difficult essay question, you might feel a little overwhelmed by the challenge. Even the most approachable and friendly professors can throw you for a loop with some of their essay questions, so don't let yourself freak out just yet! Drawing on your skill to remain calm, you can start figuring out ways to answer the essay question.

Firstly, you might want to go straight to the source, your professor. If you're puzzled by what is expected, try contacting your teacher either through email or in-person, as it is a great way to understand what they may be looking for from you. Another less stressful option is to discuss the assignment with any teacher assistant that might be assigned to the course. Even your fellow students might have some helpful input that will give you an idea of where to start. Failing that, you'll have to rely on deductive reasoning and logic to figure out an angle to focus on.

At this point, you can sit down and look at the keywords mentioned in the essay question. One important set of words is any reference to books or articles. These should be the basis for your research. Another word that you should take note of is the verb.

How to Write a Paragraph Using Study Skills

Is your teacher asking you to list, name, outline, state, or summarize? That will require something entirely different than if they want you to analyze or compare and contrast two things. We can break these kinds of questions down into four types:

Opinion

- Function: To share your opinion and prove your stance with evidence.
- Verb cues: What is your opinion about...?, Do you think...

Summary

- Function: To show that you understand the facts or information.
- Verb cues: list, name, outline, state, summarize

Analysis

- Function: To compare and contrast OR show cause and effect without stating your opinion.
- Verb cues: analyze, discuss, explain

Synthesis

- Function: To show that you can apply the ideas you learned to other situations or examples.
- Verb cues: evaluate, explain, illustrate, prove, show

Recognizing what essay is required of you will help you determine whether you're writing an informative, persuasive, argumentative, or expository essay. You'll also be able to figure out what kind of research needs to be achieved to best answer the question. Consider this essay question:

"According to Machiavelli's Prince, what are the most important qualities of a political leader? Use specific details and examples to explain why these qualities are important."

Since we are requested to use Machiavelli's famous book, we can guess that this essay is not asking for our personal opinion. This rules out opinion. We can also note that we're being asked to argue for our understanding of which qualities are important to Machiavelli. This rules out a summary-focused essay and the word 'explain' points-to analysis. Since we're being asked to propose specific qualities Machiavelli favored and to support that with examples from the text, an analysis is more than likely required. If the teacher had asked us to apply Machiavelli's ideas to a modern-day reader, that would require a synthesis style approach. However, even though you might understand what you need to do to answer the question, you still might have to figure out what direction you want to take.

Breaking it Down

With a general idea of where you want to go, it's time to break the project into achievable steps. It's a good idea to err on the side of caution and give yourself extra time, for studying and writing, just in case an emergency crops up. Sit down and draw up a rough timeline for when you should finish researching and pre-writing, and by what time you should complete the first draft, second draft, and so on. The checklist of steps for your paper should probably look like this:

- brainstorming
- pre-researching
- outlining a rough draft
- researching

- outlining a P.E.E/P.E.A-based draft
- writing the first draft
- substantive editing
- creating the second draft
- copy-editing with peer review
- finishing the third draft
- handing it in

Once you have a schedule laid out, it's time to get into the pre-writing and research phase. Just like your preparation for writing a paragraph, you will need to start with the simple steps of brainstorming, early researching, and sketching out a rough outline. Moving from the rough sketch of your ideas into a more detailed P.E.E/P.E.A-based outline will set you on the path to more efficient writing. That will allow more time for editing and polishing later on. With all of these steps laid out, you can break them down into smaller goals that you can spread throughout the coming weeks.

Organizing Larger Writing Projects

Just thinking about an essay, regardless of the minimum word count, can feel like a momentous task. However, as noted before, when you break the project down into smaller goals, you will discover that the massive essay is more achievable than you imagined! Part of the breakdown includes tackling the paper one section at a time. That is all made possible when you have a well-developed outline based on solid research and clear, logical progression. When you have the roadmap before you, you will be able to keep the big picture in mind while diving into the smaller details at the same time.

Looking at the Big Picture

One of the most important functions of an outline is to increase your ability to create flow and connectivity between ideas, whether it's argumentative, expository, or chronological. After all, you won't be able to create a smooth progression of ideas if you don't know what you're aiming for. This is why taking the time to formulate a rough outline as well as a more detailed one will give you the support you need to start writing.

Of course, for following a cause-effect or chronological order, you'll want to start at the beginning and show clear changes over time as required. On the other hand, if your paper requires argumentation or persuasion, how you order your arguments can lend more weight to the overall paper. As you create your P.E.E/P.E.A-based detailed outline, you will want to reorder your main argument points so that you start strong and end strong as well. All three of your points might be very persuasive, but if you have a weaker, less well-supported argument, you can always place it in the front, creating a WEAK-STRONG-STRONG pattern, or put it in the middle for a STRONG-WEAK-STRONG pattern. Either way, don't let your third and final point peter off uncertainly. Choose your best argument and leave it until the end, so your reader comes away feeling more persuaded and invested.

Having settled on your strongest logical progression, you can finalize your last outline and start detailing what each paragraph will contain. At this point, the last phase of research should be ending as you prepare to start writing in earnest. Now that you have settled on the logical progression of your paper, it's time to use each essay paragraph type for its intended purpose.

Paragraphs in Larger Contexts

So far, you have worked on a single paragraph that either explained, described, persuaded, or narrated a specific topic. However, as you noticed, there was a lot of talk about transition sentences. That's because, most of the time, paragraphs are part of a larger whole and need to lead the reader to the next section. That said, not all paragraphs are the same. There are three basic paragraph types to be found in an essay: introduction paragraphs, body paragraphs, and conclusion paragraphs. For a standard five-paragraph essay, you will have one introduction and conclusion paragraph and three body paragraphs. The order should be fairly obvious:

- introduction
- body paragraph
- body paragraph
- body paragraph
- conclusion

If we think about how a paragraph is formed, we can see that an essay is rather like the macro version of a paragraph. Just like how the topic and concluding sentences form the bun pieces of a hamburger, so too do the introduction and conclusion paragraphs bookend the regular academic paper. In a similar way to the detail sentences of a paragraph, the body paragraphs form the meat and salad of the hamburger model of an essay. Of course, these paragraphs each have a lot of detail within them but, the general shape of a five-paragraph essay follows this simple formula. But what happens when we zoom in on a paragraph within our essay?

Types of Paragraphs in an Essay

The three-paragraph types of an essay achieve three basic functions. Introduction paragraphs introduce the topic and state the thesis statement. Body paragraphs hold the main points that support the thesis and provide the evidence and arguments as well as the analysis and explanations required. Finally, the conclusion paragraph wraps everything up with a summary and sometimes a call to action for the reader.

Many diagrams of the hamburger model, or five-paragraph essay, might use upside-down triangles to depict what happens in the introduction and conclusion paragraphs. That's because introduction paragraphs often move from a generalized hook to a very specific, thesis-based focus, while conclusion paragraphs do the opposite. This results in a more detailed essay outline looking something like this:

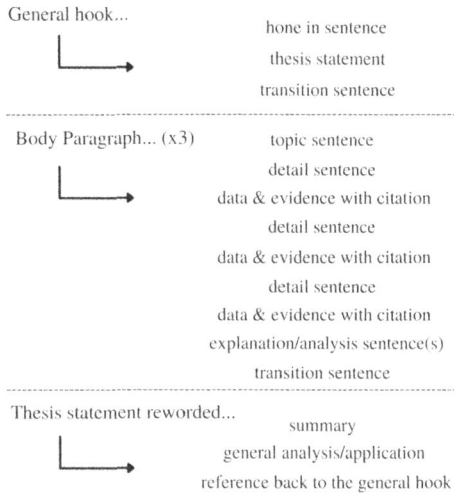

Introductions and Conclusions

Since we already know what makes up a body paragraph, let's take a closer look at the introduction and conclusion paragraphs. An introduction paragraph usually begins with a hook, also known as a sentence that catches the reader's attention. Usually, it can be a scenario, a quote, or a question. Once you create a hook, you move from more general statements to a very specific thesis sentence. Crafting a good thesis statement would probably take a chapter in and of itself to explore, but simply put, a thesis contains all of the information in the three arguments you're proposing. That is to say; there should be no surprises as to what the reader will find in the body paragraphs in general. For example, a beginner essay writer might propose a thesis stating, "I love fall because the weather is so atmospheric, the excitement around the start of a new school year is inspiring, and the holiday festivities are super fun!". As you can guess, the following three paragraphs will center around weather, the school year, and the autumn holidays. Overall, suppose a paragraph has a minimum of five sentences in it. In that case, you might want to allocate one to the hook, one to a general (transition) statement, one or two for the thesis, and then one for a transition sentence.

The conclusion paragraph of an essay is not much different as it's simply reversed. The first sentence may be a transition statement that leads to a rewording of the thesis. From there, the writer may analyze, synthesize, or summarize takeaway points or some form of practical application. Then, the essay may end with a reference back to the starting hook, or encouragement, for the reader. Once again, this paragraph need not be more than five sentences, or so, giving the reader a sense of conclusion and investment without overstaying its welcome. With that, your essay is done!

With this in mind, you can see that there's an obvious formula to writing a basic essay. However, in later levels of study as well as in professional arenas, this formula may be changed to fit a variety of academic or professional requirements. Additional paragraphs may be added to discuss topics that aren't addressed, or there might be too much information for each point to be in a single paragraph. Furthermore, some essays will require more than three arguments or will need a branched set of argumentation to follow. Either way, if you're a beginner or someone who wants to revisit the fundamentals of writing, following this simple model for an essay is a great start to get you writing!

Fiction and Non-fiction Differences

Unlike non-fiction writing projects, fiction might appear to be free from the helpful guidelines of an outline, but that doesn't have to be the case. Even narrative fiction relies on formulas or alternative versions of age-old story progression. Some of the earliest story cycles, like the hero's journey, remain popular today!

If you're an architectural writer, you will already find yourself jotting down lists or plotting narrative outlines, deciding when and how certain story beats will happen. Something as simple as the "plot mountain," which outlines the introduction, buildup, climax, and resolution of a story, can guide any writer through the bare bones of their story idea. A story's general outline might look something like this:

- buildup
- first climax
- more buildup
- final climax
- resolution

Depending on the genre, outlines may look more simple or more complex. Romance and horror fiction, for example, require particular beats and organization to keep the pace familiar and interesting for their invested readers. For some writers who aim to tackle a series, the study skills: organization, time management, and appropriate research allow them to create suspenseful foreshadowing and complex plots that can span multiple books.

Unfortunately, not all writers lean toward organization naturally. Thankfully, like all study skills, using paragraphs within more extensive outlines is an ability any writer can develop over time. With the help of organization and logical progression, the challenges of writer's block, and plot holes, can more easily be tackled.

What You Need To Remember

Whether you're facing an academic paper, a daily blog post, or the next big fantasy series, you can rely on the study skills and writing techniques discussed in this book. With the help of schedules, routines, and supportive environments, you'll discover that you're more empowered than ever to tackle any writing project you want. With the proper use of time management and outlines, your ideas will no longer be challenged by procrastination, writer's block, or lack of ideas. Do you want to be trapped indoors staring out at the sky, wishing you were doing something else? No? I didn't think so either. Thankfully, you don't have to waste unnecessary time and energy on writing. Instead, maximize your time and mental power with the tips and techniques mentioned in this book. You're now ready to write anything you want!

In Summary

Top Tip: Break Large Tasks into Smaller Achievable Ones!

Rome wasn't built in a single day. The same goes for any writing project you're taking on. The more complex the project, the longer it will take, especially the research and pre-writing phases. That being said, don't give up! Instead, be patient with yourself and give yourself time to organize your study plan and writing process. When you break the project down into manageable parts, you will discover that you can rise to the challenge and write something that will catch your readers' eye. It all starts with the first small step.

Challenge!

Starting with the paragraph you completed earlier, how would it work in a larger writing project? Is it blog material, or would it work as part of an essay?

You might want to try writing a larger piece using your completed paragraph as a jumping-off point. You might also want to use these customizable writing prompts to practice writing paragraphs or five-paragraph essays!

- Discuss or describe your favorite season.
- Compare and contrast two items, books, or films.
- Write a book report.
- Try to summarize an event for a friend.
- Share a childhood experience.
- Argue for a specific response to a socio-cultural situation.

Snapshot

Essays, particularly higher-level academic papers, offer a complicated challenge to most writers. However, after you take time analyzing the essay question and figure out the direction you feel confident to explore, it's time to brainstorm and order your main ideas or arguments into a logical progression that will keep your reader invested. Once you have outlined the entire paper in detail, you can start writing. Still, keep in mind that paragraphs change depending on their placement in the paper, such as introduction and conclusion paragraphs. The good news is there are ways to approach these paragraphs, just as there are formulas for essay outlines. Going forward, whether you're writing fiction or non-fiction, you now understand how study skills can provide you with the organization and motivation you need to overcome procrastination, plot holes, and writer's block!

Conclusion

Imagine. It's another beautiful, sunny summer day, and you're heading out to your car again. You're planning to meet up with a friend for some drinks on a restaurant patio. Where? You're not sure whether you know the location they chose or not, but that's fine. After all, you have a newfound ability—you're able to find any place you desire! Inside your memory lies a magical map that can bring you to any destination you choose, regardless of your starting point. Your map is customized to your own particular needs, ready to take you anywhere, and always get you there on time.

Sounds too good to be true? It isn't! After working through this book, you now have a roadmap for any writing project that might be challenging you. When you pick up your class syllabus, glance over your boss's proposal, plan your next month of blog posts, or start to compose an email, you will already know what you have to do!

Your Own Road Map

Facing a deadline no longer has to overwhelm you or stress you out. Instead, you now understand how to use study skills to manage your time and schedule a study plan for yourself. After creating a supportive study environment and developing healthy study habits, you're better able to tackle the writing projects you face.

Next, following the steps discussed in this book, you'll be able to craft any kind of paragraph, whether it's part of a larger whole or not. Remember, start by considering your audience and how that will affect your writing. Then, you will formulate a rough outline that will guide your research. After further reading and searching, your finalized outline will provide you with the details and notes you need to get started. Now it's time to get writing. However, after getting the first draft done, you'll

Conclusion

undoubtedly notice errors and mistakes cropping up everywhere.

At this point, don't panic! This is normal for every single writer on the planet. What comes next involves two stages of corrections: substantive editing and copy-editing. During the substantive editing phase, you can rethink the logical organization of your ideas, target weak points in your research, and rewrite large portions of paragraphs as needed. The next phase, copy-editing, will be the extra polish that makes every piece of writing legible and easy to read. It's at this point that you might be struggling to remain focused and motivated, but with the four proofreading techniques provided in this book, you'll be able to prepare your final draft. Your writing is now ready to be shared with the world!

The Broad Horizon Before You

Look back on the road you have traveled so far. You started this journey worrying about how you were going to complete your writing assignment. Perhaps you were someone who had years of experience battling with the blank page. Maybe you kept feeling overwhelmed by the blog post your boss needed you

Conclusion

to write. Deep down, you might have been wondering whether writing was a gift, and you just didn't have it. Whatever the case, you can move forward assured that you have the strengths, skills, and techniques to handle whatever gets thrown at you. Your dreams of writing that book you always wanted might have seemed impossible to achieve. The essay deadline your professor announced might have appeared daunting. Your child's writing assignment may have even challenged how far you could have helped them... But that's all about to change. Now that you're empowered to pave your own road, take the wheel, and speed off to the horizon you want to chase!

Scan the QR code below to claim your free copy of the '*5 Habits that make Learning any Subject Quicker and Easier*' plus bonus content!

About the Author

Stephanie Reeves has an extensive background in psychology and currently works in childcare and education with young people with various needs, including learning disabilities, autism, and typical developmental difficulties. She trains at postgraduate level in the field of psychoanalytic psychotherapy for children and adolescents to support the emotional, educational, and developmental needs of families and individuals who are struggling.

Stephanie Reeves has a keen interest in child development and human behavior. Through her work, she strives to provide skills to children and young people that they can use throughout their lives. She believes that every individual should have the right tools to help them in areas they struggle with regardless of their background or ability!

Helping you achieve success in writing skills matters deeply to Stephanie Reeves because they are invaluable life skills. Learning to write means learning the skills to communicate effectively, which you can use throughout school, college, and the adult world. Through working, volunteering, and studying in different countries, including Sri Lanka and Thailand, Stephanie Reeves has a breadth of expertise in applying writing techniques to various skill-set levels in individuals.

Stephanie Reeves' background in working within a psychologically reflective framework has also helped her understand students' and learners' specific difficulties. Through reflecting on the methods and techniques that work for each person, she has been able to skillfully support them to make learning simple, fun, and engaging.

Scan the QR code to join our Facebook group,
English Writing Tools, *and become a part of the community!*

If you've enjoyed 'How to Write a Paragraph Using Study Skills: 5 Simple Steps to Writing Powerful Paragraphs', please leave a review using the QR code below. Your feedback will be greatly appreciated!

- Steph

Glossary

Active verb: When the subject is the one driving the action, the verb is active. Sometimes the subject is doing something to a direct object or can be further described in terms of time and place, but the latter is not necessary.

- Example: *'The brown kitten jumped.'*
- Example: *'The brown kitten jumped onto the dog.'*

Adjective: Most adjectives are words that help describe or add details to nouns, but some can also be used to modify adverbs and other parts of speech. Many adjectives are found right before the nouns they're modifying, but some can be found after linking or stative verbs.

- Example: *'The red, bouncy ball fell down the stairs.'*
- Example: *'The ball is red and bouncy.'*

Antonym: Opposite to a synonym, an antonym is defined as the opposite of a word. For example, if you're looking up the word 'tall,' an antonym you might find would be 'short.'

Call to action: Many blogs and marketing may have a section dedicated to the "call to action" for the reader. In this part of the blog, the reader won't only receive practical applications to consider, in light of the information they just read, but also resources or other ways to respond to the information. A call to action may include an opportunity to interact with the writer's brand as well, such as buying a book or downloading free material.

Citations: For academic or professional writing, sources are often required as proof of data or evidence for the writer's argument or report. Citations are included in-text and in a reference list at the end. Depending on the situation and academic field, different styles of referencing are required, such as APA, MLA, and CMS.

Connotation: The secondary meaning of a word. Often defined by another idea or feeling that is connected to that word over time. For example, a person may refer to someone as being overweight or full-figured if they want to communicate neutrality or positivity. Other derogatory words will have more negative connotations and, in many writing cases, should be avoided as much as possible.

Copy-editing: This involves small-scale, detailed editing that focuses on grammar, spelling, and punctuation.

Denotation: A word's literal and primary meaning, as is usually understood within specific contexts. For example, everyone should recognize that the words' smart,' 'clever,' 'wise,' and 'crafty' are linked to the general meaning of being intelligent.

Ideate: to imagine, conceive or think of an idea

In-text citation: When a writer summarizes or directly quotes a source, in-text citations are required to note where the idea or fact came from.

Glossary

Fiction: Writing, whether prose or poetry, that's not based on real-life events. Most fiction novels and stories are based on imaginary events and people.

Fluff (waffling): When attempting to reach a specific word count, writers might fill paragraphs with overly complex sentences or unnecessary sentences that restate information in a different way. Also known as padding, this is to be avoided at all costs.

Logical fallacy: These are flawed or deceptive arguments that can undermine the information you're sharing. While some fallacies are useful when used thoughtfully, most should be avoided: including the false dilemma, the slippery slope, and the strawman argument.

Mind map: This form of brainstorming uses circles connected by lines to stimulate a student or writer's ability to connect ideas and find patterns.

Non-fiction: Writing, whether prose or poetry, based on real-life events or that relates to information or data. Cookbooks, essays, and textbooks are just some examples of non-fiction.

Noun: A noun is a person, place, or thing. Those that name a specific person, place, or thing are called proper nouns, while unspecified nouns are known as common nouns.

- Example of proper nouns: '*Carmen lives in Paris.*'
- Example of common nouns: '*My sister dropped her laptop at school.*'

Noun-verb agreement: When writing in English (and some other languages), nouns and verbs have to 'agree' or match. For example, many verbs will lose an 's' if the noun is plural.

- Example: '*The dog gnaws on the bone.*'
- Example: '*The dogs gnaw on the bones.*'

Outline: The bones of your writing project. Outlines provide a framework that you can follow along as you write.

Passive verb: When the subject is receiving an action from a direct object, or indirect object, the verb being used is more than likely passive. When passive verbs are used, there are almost always other parts of speech following the verb.

- Example: '*The ball was thrown by a young boy onto the roof.*'

Paragraph: Focuses on a single idea or argument. Paragraphs provide a single point, some evidence, and the following analysis or explanations. There are four types of paragraphs in terms of function: narrative, descriptive, expository, and persuasive. However, in a large work of writing, paragraph types can also change in form depending on their roles, such as introductory, body, and conclusion paragraphs.

Sentence: A group of words that creates a complete thought. Complete sentences require a subject and predicate. Divided into four types, sentences are either: statements, questions, exclamations, or commands. However, in a paragraph, the focus and function of a sentence may change depending on its placement. Topic and thesis sentences determine the focus of the paragraph/writing project, while detail or evidence sentences carry the information. Conclusion or transition sentences wrap up the paragraph or sometimes signal the next.

Sentence structure: There are four main sentence structures: simple, complex, compound, and compound-complex. Depending on which sentence structure we're talking about, there must be at least one subject and one verb (predicate) with some requiring subordinate (or dependent) clauses.

- Example of a simple sentence: '*Emma ran down the street quickly.*'
- Example of a complex sentence: '*Emma ran down the street quickly as she looked for her cat.*'
- Example of a compound sentence: '*Emma ran down the street quickly, but she didn't see any sign of her cat.*'
- Example of a compound-complex sentence: '*Emma ran down the street quickly, but she didn't see any sign of her cat, which really bummed her out.*' (Sources: See citations.)

Subject: A noun or short clause that does the action in a sentence. Sometimes, a sentence will have two or more nouns, but most are found toward the beginning of a sentence regardless of how many subjects are mentioned.

- Example: '*Mary-Sue and Danni arrived at school ten minutes late.* '

Glossary

- Example: '*At the sight of the fireworks, everyone clapped and cheered.*'
- Example: '*Knowing is not the same as doing.*'

Substantive editing: This form of editing involves major content changes as it requires you to tweak the organization of a written work and supplement information as required. If you're adding more points or evidence to a paragraph or removing fluff, this counts as substantive editing.

Synonym: A synonym refers to a word that is similar in meaning to another word. This doesn't mean that their connotations are the same. Instead, they share a link in terms of their literal, primary meaning. For example, the words' dismal,' 'somber,' and 'pessimistic' are all tied to the word 'sad.'

Thesis: A thesis is a sentence or a group of sentences that define(s) the general focus and argument of an academic paper. This statement guides the 'aim' of the paper and must be supported by evidence and data with appropriate sourcing and citations. Most thesis statements are found toward the end of the introductory paragraph of an essay.

Transition words/phrases: When moving from one idea to another, they help smooth the flow and signal to the reader a change is going to happen. This may include adding more details, contrasting with another idea, or even signaling the next step of an event.

Verb: The word(s) used to show action or statement of being in a sentence are called verbs. Like many other languages, English verbs will change to indicate time or reflect the plurality of nouns. Some verbs are action verbs, while others are stative or linking ('is,' 'am,' 'are'). Depending on how a verb is used in a sentence, it may also change from active to passive.

References

1. Arthur Conan Doyle. (2022). *The complete Sherlock Holmes*. Sherlock-Holm.es. https://sherlock-holm.es/stories/html/cano.html
2. Bauer-Ramazani, C. (2019). *Essay questions*. Saint Michael's College. http://academics.smcvt.edu/cbauer-ramazani/IEP/acad_skills/essay_questions.htm#:~:text=Answer%20the%20question%20according%20to
3. Broderick, T. (2020, August 24). *How to study with dyslexia and dysgraphia*. Affordable Colleges Online. https://www.affordablecollegesonline.org/college-resource-center/dyslexia-dysgraphia/
4. Bunton, C. (2020, May 13). *Best upcoming*

References

folding phones 2020: Top flexible phones to look forward to. Pocket-Lint. https://www.pocket-lint.com/phones/news/151418-best-upcoming-foldable-phones

5. Children's Educational Services. (2020, July 26). *Five tips for helping students with special needs*. CES Schools. https://www.ces-schools.net/five-tips-for-helping-students-with-special-needs/

6. College Internship Program. (2021). *10 tips to help you stay focused: for students with autism and learning differences*. College Internship Program. https://info.cipworld-wide.org/blog/10-tips-to-help-you-stay-focused

7. Collins, K. (2020). *Strategies/techniques for ADHD*. The Division of Disability Resources & Educational Services. https://www.disability.illinois.edu/strategiestechniques-adhd

8. Cottrell, S. (2019). The study skills handbook. In *Google Books*. Macmillan International Higher Education.

9. CSO at the Movies. (2019). *Two notes that changed the film world: John Williams' theme for "Jaws" - CSO Sounds & Stories*.

References

Chicago Symphony Orchestra. https://csosoundsandstories.org/two-notes-that-changed-the-film-world-john-williams-theme-for-jaws/

10. Dolin, A. (2014, January 14). *7 secrets to studying better with ADHD*. ADDitude. https://www.additudemag.com/learn-more-in-less-time/

11. Duistermaat, H. (2017, June 20). *How to spot 8 weaknesses in your writing (and fix them)*. Enchanting Marketing. https://www.enchantingmarketing.com/writing-weaknesses/

12. Education Corner. (2021). *Study skills guide: find an effective study location*. Www.educationcorner.com. https://www.educationcorner.com/study-location.html

13. Foster, M. B. (2021). Powerful verbs for weaving ideas in essays. In The University of Arizona. https://salt.arizona.edu/sites/salt.arizona.edu/files/tutoringfiles/handouts/Powerful%20Verbs%20for%20Essays.pdf

14. Foundation for Critical Thinking, The. (2017). *Defining Critical Thinking*. Criticalthinking.org. https://www.criticalthinking.org/pages/defining-critical-thinking/766

References

15. GetLitt. (2019, November 4). *Paragraph writing for kids*. GetLitt! https://www.getlitt.co/blog/paragraph-writing-for-kids/
16. Gettinger, M., & Seibert, J. K. (2002). Contributions of study skills to academic competence. *School Psychology Review*
17. Harvard Writing Center. (2019). *Outlining*. Harvard.edu. https://writingcenter.fas.harvard.edu/pages/outlining
18. History.com Editors. (2009). *Nikola Tesla*. History. https://www.history.com/topics/inventions/nikola-tesla
19. Indeed Editorial Team. (2021, February 22). *How to write a topic sentence (with examples and tips)*. Indeed Career Guide. https://www.indeed.com/career-advice/career-development/how-to-write-a-topic-sentence
20. Indiana University Bloomington. (2019). *Paragraphs & topic sentences*. Writing Tutorial Services. https://wts.indiana.edu/writing-guides/paragraphs-and-topic-sentences.html
21. Intelligent. (2013). *Create a study plan*. Intelligent. https://www.intelligent.com/create-a-study-plan/

References

22. Jackson State Community College. (2021). *Five-Paragraph essay*. Jackson State Community College. https://www.jscc.edu/academics/programs/writing-center/writing-resources/five-paragraph-essay.html

23. Kampen, D. V. (2019). *LibGuides: writing help (formatting, templates, and writing samples): sample bad and good paragraphs*. Slulibrary.saintleo.edu. https://slulibrary.saintleo.edu/c.php?g=367733&p=2485890

24. Kelly, K. (2020). *7 study tips to help grade-schoolers with dyslexia*. Www.understood.org. https://www.understood.org/articles/en/7-study-tips-to-help-grade-schoolers-with-dyslexia

25. Kemp, G., Smith, M., & Segal, J. (2019, March 20). *Helping children with learning disabilities*. HelpGuide. https://www.helpguide.org/articles/autism-learning-disabilities/helping-children-with-learning-disabilities.htm

26. Kenas, J. (2021, August 23). *Types of paragraphs: based on writing, structure and format*. LearnPar. https://learnpar.com/types-of-paragraphs/

References

27. Learn American English Online. (2012). *Types of paragraphs*. Learn American English Online. https://www.learnamericanenglishonline.com/Write_in_English/WL10_types_of_paragraphs.html
28. Ledohowski, L. (2021). *PEE: The secret to writing a good paragraph.* Www.essayjack.com. https://www.essayjack.com/blog/the-secret-to-writing-a-good-paragraph
29. Linford, J. (2014). *Essay planning: outlining with a purpose.* https://www.sjsu.edu/writingcenter/docs/handouts/Essay%20-Planning%20-%20Outlining.pdf
30. Loveless, B. (2019). *Study habits of highly effective students*. Educationcorner.com. https://www.educationcorner.com/habits-of-successful-students.html
31. Low, K. (2019). *How students with ADHD can be successful in college*. Verywell Mind. https://www.verywellmind.com/college-students-with-adhd-20820
32. McCombes, S. (2019, January 21). *How to write topic sentences*. Scribbr. https://www.scribbr.com/research-

References

paper/topic-sentences/#:~:text=A%20-good%20topic%20sentence%20is

33. Moreno, S. (2018, October 18). *A teacher's brief guide to teaching students with high-functioning autism*. Reading Rockets. https://www.readingrockets.org/article/teacher-s-brief-guide-teaching-students-high-functioning-autism

34. Open Book Bag, The. (2021). *Four functions of paragraphs*. Www.openbookbag.com. http://openbookbag.com/4function.html

35. Pattern Based Writing. (2011, February 28). *Paragraph examples: expository, narrative, persuasive, descriptive, and more*. Pattern Based Writing: Quick & Easy Essay. https://patternbasedwriting.com/elementary_writing_success/paragraph-examples/

36. Purdue Writing Lab. (2018). *On paragraphs*. Purdue Writing Lab. https://owl.purdue.edu/owl/general_writing/academic_writing/paragraphs_and_paragraphing/index.html

37. Schiller, A., & Boisvert, M. (2019, October 30). *4 main types of procrastinators, and how to avoid being one*. Business Insider. https://www.businessinsider.com/main-types-

References

of-procrastinators-how-to-avoid-accountability-coaches

38. SkillsYouNeed. (2011). *Study skills*. Skillsyouneed.com. https://www.skillsyouneed.com/learn/study-skills.html
39. Stephen York Editorial Services. (2016, June 30). *Tips for writers: how to cut the waffle*. Stephen York Editorial Services. https://yorkeditorial.com/2016/06/30/tips-for-writers-how-to-cut-the-waffle/
40. Stetson University. (2021). *Planning a better study schedule*. https://www.stetson.edu/administration/academic-success/media/STUDY%20SCHEDULE.pdf
41. Taylor, C., & Blinka, D. (2021, September 16). *How to structure paragraphs in an essay*. WikiHow. https://www.wikihow.com/Structure-Paragraphs-in-an-Essay
42. Teachingwithoutfrills. (2018, November 6). *How to write for your audience*. Www.youtube.com. https://www.youtube.com/watch?v=PTD_EZWCO7w
43. Twinkl. (2021). *Paragraph*. Twinkl.ca. https://www.twinkl.ca/teaching-wiki/paragraph
44. University of Birmingham. (2021). *A short*

References

guide to paragraph structure. University of Birmingham. https://intranet.birmingham.ac.uk/as/libraryservices/library/asc/resources/a-short-guide-to-paragraph-structure.aspx

45. University of Maryland. (2019). *Writing for an audience.* Umgc.edu. https://www.umgc.edu/current-students/learning-resources/writing-center/writing-resources/getting-started-writing/writing-for-an-audience.cfm

46. University of Nebraska-Lincoln. (2021). *Editing: analyzing your writing strengths and weaknesses.* Researchwriting.unl.edu. https://researchwriting.unl.edu/editing-analyzing-your-writing-strengths-and-weaknesses

47. University of North Caroline at Chapel Hill, The. (2019). *Editing and proofreading.* The Writing Center. https://writingcenter.unc.edu/tips-and-tools/editing-and-proofreading/

48. University of Washington. (2021). *Paragraph function.* Depts.washington.edu. https://depts.washington.edu/pswrite/parafunct.html

49. Wali, O., & Madani, Q. A. (2020). The importance of paragraph writing: an

References

introduction. In *International Journal of Latest Research in Humanities and Social Science*. http://www.ijlrhss.com/paper/volume-3-issue-7/7-HSS-704.pdf

50. Writerwithagoal. (2014, July 3). *What are your strengths and weaknesses with writing?* Writing Prompts for Rookie Writers. https://writingpromptsforrookiewriters.wordpress.com/2014/07/03/what-are-your-strengths-and-weaknesses-with-writing/

51. World Bank Group, The. (2012). *Identify good and bad paragraphs*. Colelearning.net. http://colelearning.net/rw_wb/module5/page5.html

52. Yale Center for Dyslexia and Creativity, The. (2017). *Tips From Students*. Yale Dyslexia. https://dyslexia.yale.edu/resources/dyslexic-kids-adults/tips-from-students/

53. Yamin, Moh. (2019). Learning from students' experiences in writing paragraph. *Metathesis: Journal of English Language, Literature, and Teaching, 3*(2), 188. https://doi.org/10.31002/metathesis.v3i2.1736

Made in the USA
Las Vegas, NV
17 October 2023